Beyond the Reef

Records of the Conference of Churches and Missions in the Pacific

Malua Theological College
Western Samoa

22nd April – 4th May 1961

Published by the
International Missionary Council
on behalf of the
Conference of Churches and Missions in the Pacific

London 1961

Printed in Great Britain by
John Roberts Press Limited
London

CONTENTS

CONTENTS

The First Conference of Churches and Missions in the Pacific

In February, 1959, the International Missionary Council was invited by a number of churches and missions in the Pacific area to organize a conference of churches and missions in that area. A sense of need for such a meeting had been increasingly apparent in the area, and consultation by correspondence initiated by the London Missionary Society with churches and missions in the Pacific had shown it to be a widely shared need. The Pacific area was not immune to the economic, social and political changes taking place in the world. Those changes were putting questions to the churches about their own life and about their responsibilities towards the communities in which they were set. They were feeling the need for consultation together to learn from one another's experience and to think together about the responsibilities they shared towards the Pacific area.

The International Missionary Council readily responded to this request, which is entirely in line with one of its primary purposes, and undertook the task of organizing a conference. The nature of the Conference desired had been indicated in the initial request from the churches and missions, for instance that it should be a small study conference and that its programme should be so planned as to allow ample time for informal conversation, in which the churches and missions in the area, through their appointed representatives, could come to know something about one another's life and work. Certain subjects which were engaging their thought were suggested as topics for the Conference.

Preliminary correspondence with the churches and missions in the area showed a general desire to participate in such a conference and a willingness to give time and thought to preparing for it by Bible study and discussion of its themes in the churches. Advantage was taken of a journey of the General Secretary of the International Missionary Council to Australia to convene in Suva, Fiji, in March, 1960, a small group of advisers from different geographical areas and from different church traditions to advise the International Missionary Council on organizational matters and the content and arrangement of the programme; the actual programme of the Conference (see p. 11) followed very closely the lines suggested by this advisory group.

In preparation for the Conference, the participating churches and missions were invited to undertake three activities. They were asked to discuss the themes of the Conference, not so much in specially convened meetings as in the regular meetings taking place in their own church life. For this purpose, a series of notes and questions for discussion on the five topics chosen for the Conference was provided. Secondly, they were asked to undertake, over a period, study of the Letter to the Galatians which was to be the basis of Bible Study at the Conference. Thirdly, they were asked to pray for the Conference, and a prayer leaflet with a daily prayer for the Conference was printed and widely circulated.

This preparatory work was taken seriously by the churches and missions sharing in the Conference. The fact that it was widely and responsibly undertaken had three important consequences. There is a good deal of testimony to the stimulating effect of this process of self-examination in the light of the questions addressed to the churches on the Conference themes, and especially in the light of the study of the Letter to the Galatians. Further, the process resulted in the churches feeling really engaged in the Conference; it was an event which involved them and to which their own thought and prayer and Bible study were contributing. Finally, their representatives shared in the Conference not merely as individuals, but with some understanding of the mind of their churches on the themes discussed and with some preparation for engagement with others in corporate Bible study. The readiness with which the Conference attained a real sense of common purpose would not have been possible without this responsible participation in common preparation within the several churches.

The churches in Samoa (the Samoan Church (L.M.S.) and the Methodist Church in Samoa) invited the Conference to meet in Samoa, and this invitation was accepted. The buildings of the Malua Theological College of the Samoan Church were put at the disposal of the Conference and provided most admirable accommodation in a beautiful setting. The two churches generously gave hospitality for the members of the Conference, and this was provided by their women's organizations, a different district taking responsibility on each day of the Conference and caring for the needs of its members with a gracious and generous thoughtfulness that made a great contribution to its work. On the two Sundays members of the Conference visited neighbouring congregations in pairs. A *Kava* ceremony on the Saturday, shared in by the leaders of government in both Eastern and Western Samoa, an evening in which the Conference members were entertained with a zestful display of Samoan songs and dances both traditional and contemporary, and the entertainment of those who spent a night en route to or from the Conference in Pagopago in Eastern Samoa enabled the Conference to share something of Samoan life and culture. All these arrangements, made by a local arrangements committee under the chairmanship of the Rev. Vavae Toma, Secretary of the Samoan Church (L.M.S.), combined to assure the Conference that it was most warmly welcomed by the churches in Samoa, while ensuring it of the leisure of time and mind to enable it to do its work. A small indication of what its members felt about this thoughtful and generous provision for its needs will be found in the Conference's resolutions of appreciation (p. 102).

The representatives who gathered at Malua on Friday and Saturday, 21st and 22nd April, represented not only widely scattered churches but churches set in very diverse situations. Most of them had undertaken journeys over great distances to be present (though the length of time occupied by the journeys varied according to whether or not air travel was available rather than to the distance covered). The travel costs of all the representatives were met by the churches or missions they represented: in many instances churches had raised special funds involving most generous giving by their members to enable their representatives to attend—one of many indications that the Conference was an event which they regarded as of real importance to their life and work. They came from an area extending from Western New Guinea to Tahiti, and from such diverse situations as that in Samoa—where the long established church is almost coterminous with the community, to the Highlands of New Guinea—where first contacts between the church and hitherto isolated tribes are still taking place. They came from the Anglican, Baptist, Congregational, Lutheran, Methodist, and Presbyterian-Reformed traditions of churchmanship. In addition to the 55 representatives of the churches and missions in the Pacific area, there were observers appointed by the main mission boards working in the area, and consultants from the International Missionary Council, the World Council of Churches, the East Asia Christian Conference, and the Hawaiian Evangelical Association of Congregational Christian Churches. (A list of participants will be found on p. 107.)

The five topics chosen for the Conference's discussion were: —
    The ministry;
    The unfinished evangelistic task ;
    The relevance of the Gospel to the changing conditions of life in
      the Pacific ;
    The place of young people in the life of the Church ;
    The Christian family.
These were opened out in plenary session by two speeches on each, one by someone from within the area and a second by a consultant from outside it. They were then discussed by five Commissions, as widely representative as possible of the different geographical areas and church traditions. The reports of the Commissions were then presented in plenary session, which discussed, amended and "received" them. (For the reports of the Commissions see pp. 84-99.)

In considering these topics in preparation for the Conference, the advisory group had discerned that beneath them there lay a more fundamental issue. It had this to say about it to the churches: —

"In the days before the coming of the Gospel, men's lives were ruled largely by fear. The coming of Christianity wrought a marvellous change in the life of our peoples. But we have to ask, 'Did the coming of Christianity mean that fear was replaced by love, or did it mean that men transferred their fear to a new object and began to fear God with a pagan fear?' . . . Our churches often seem to be more governed by fear than by love, more concerned to enforce conformity to certain laws of behaviour than to show their love to God by loving and forgiving others. It sometimes seems that our churches are places where certain standards are demanded, rather than places where God gives sinners forgiveness and victory over sin. It does not always seem that in our churches we expect the fruit of the presence of the Holy Spirit—love, joy, peace. . . ."

The Bible Study at the Conference proved to be the backbone of its work and may well be one of its most enduring contributions to the life of the churches. It will be seen from the programme that an hour and a half of each morning was allocated to Bible Study. It therefore provided the basis for all the rest of the Conference's discussions and sharing of news. The Rev. Hans-Ruedi Weber, who led the Bible Study, used a variety of methods in his exposition, calling to the aid of verbal exposition blackboard sketches, conversation with one's neighbour on the answer to a given question, and mime to bring out the essential message of the Letter to the Galatians. Each exposition provided a background for the discussion in small groups of a sharply pointed question, to be answered in the light of a specific passage in Galatians. The result was a confrontation, through corporate study of the Bible, of the contemporary life of the churches with the Word of God as He spoke to us through the witness of the Letter to the Galatians. This it seemed was a new experience for the great majority of representatives from the Pacific churches, who were familiar with preaching and exposition, but not with corporate Bible study in groups confronted with questions in the form: "What is God saying to us through this passage in our present actual situation?". The experience at Malua of listening together to what God is saying now through the Bible may well spread in the churches in the Pacific area. If it does, it will quicken and deepen the process, already taking place in many of the churches, of seeking reform and renewal of church life in the light of God's living Word.

One of the purposes of the Conference was to provide an opportunity for the churches in the area, so long isolated from one another by great distances and poor communications, to get to know one another and through their representatives to share something of one another's life. For this purpose the programme provided for a number of "news sessions". News of the churches in the Pacific area, collected from different geographical areas, was presented in a variety of ways by the representatives present from those areas. Some information was also given about developments in the churches in Asia, Africa and Europe, and about the International Missionary Council, the World Council of Churches and the East Asia Christian Conference. Thus in Conference sessions the members of the Conference had a new understanding of the place of the churches within the Christian community in the Pacific area and saw that community in the wider context of a Christian community which is world-wide. But the sharing of news and experiences was by no means confined to formal sessions ; it continued over meals and in bedrooms (shared by four people of different geographical areas and different church traditions) with a vigour which left no doubt of the eagerness of the participants to use to the full this opportunity to get to know each other and to learn from one another.

To at least one participant, it seemed that the Conference had a growing sense that it was God who had brought its members together, and that the Conference was an event which He desired to happen at this particular point in history. This sense found expression in the setting in worship of the Conference's activities. Morning and evening prayers, conducted by four members in four different church traditions, provided a framework of worship for its daily work. For most members of the Conference, the central act of worship during their stay at Malua was an observance of the Sacrament of the Lord's Supper held by the Samoan Church (L.M.S.) in which that church and its congregation at Malua invited the members of the Conference to join. The church used on this occasion the liturgy of the Church of South India, and the service gave all who shared in it a great sense of offering the whole work of the Conference to God in penitent thanksgiving for His gift of Jesus Christ.

What will result from the Conference? That no one can tell at present. There was an unmistakable desire amongst the members of the Conference, voiced particularly by those who were "indigenous inhabitants of the area", that having "discovered" one another and experienced a common life together, means should be provided through which this common life could continue to find expression and extension. The Conference decided to set up a Continuation Committee, and elected a Committee which is widely representative both geographically and confessionally. This Committee got down to work immediately the Conference concluded, while the first part of the "air lift" of Conference members to Pagopago was proceeding and made plans for each of its members to carry further work on one of the topics considered at the Conference, and for a further meeting of the Continuation Committee in a year's time. The Conference also decided to ask the help of the International Missionary Council in enabling this Committee to meet and in providing a secretary to further its work and the links between the churches in the area. (The relevant resolutions will be found on p. 100.)

Whether or not this organizational outcome proves to be important and creative will depend on how far it is the expression of something that lies at a deeper level. If a Continuation Committee were to be simply the result of the desire of a group of people who had enjoyed the experience of meeting together not to disperse without being able to say they had "done something" then its effectiveness would be minimal. Those who were present at Malua would, however, affirm that the decision to set up a Continuation Committee represented something much more profound than this. It may not be an exaggeration of their experience to say that this decision reflected their conviction that God was drawing His people in the Pacific into a new "togetherness" and that the provision of some means to continue the work of the Conference was a simple act of obedience to what they had discerned together of His will for His churches.

Such a conviction is not without support from the fact that the Conference actually took place and from what happened at it. Even with the help of modern transport facilities, not a few obstacles were encountered in arranging for the Conference; the fact that each of them was taken out of the path as the time of the Conference drew near is not without meaning. The thoroughness with which the churches shared in the preparatory work, and the readiness of the participating bodies to provide the travel costs, already mentioned above, are signs of something at work in the churches in the area not to be lightly dismissed. Both in the preparation and in the Conference itself one had a strong sense that this was a timely event. Increasingly the people of the area are meeting one another in "secular" contexts, for instance through travel for employment or for education, and through inter-governmental conferences. It is high time that the Christians amongst them came to know and recognize each other as members of the people of God. Increasingly, as the reports of the Commissions clearly show, they are experiencing changes in and challenges to their traditional modes of life, as this contracting world cracks the shell of their former isolation. The churches need one another if they are to discover and transmit a discriminating Christian judgment on the old and the new.

Reflecting on the Conference and its outcome, it seems, to this observer at least, that its result may be summed up in a question which it is putting to the churches and missions in the Pacific. It is a question which will be put in a variety of ways—through the reports of the Commissions, in so far as these are seriously studied and acted on in the churches and missions in the area; through the activities of the Continuation Committee; most of all perhaps through what the representatives gathered at Malua say and do in their own churches in the days ahead. At the centre of all these there will, as it seems to the present writer, be one question, put in many forms. It is this: "Are we, as churches, discovering afresh and in terms of our contemporary situation that we are the 'sent community' of the people of God?". The "sent community"—not the total community engaged in its religious exercises, but the community of God sent into the total community, and holding a responsibility not to preserve that community as it is, but to be the instrument of its redemption and recreation; the "sent community", not just the recipient of the activities of missions, but itself part of the total Christian mission in the world; the "sent community" that lives not from itself or to itself, but from the grace of God who created it in the costly gift of Jesus Christ and for the world for whose salvation its Lord gave His life. The Malua Conference will indeed have been part of the purpose of God if through it and through what flows from it, the churches and missions hear more clearly their Lord's word to them: "As the Father sent me into the world, even so send I you".

R. K. Orchard
2nd June, 1961

Programme of the Conference

Arrival   A few delegates travelled direct to Samoa, but the majority travelled via Fiji. A special flight was arranged between Nadi, Fiji and Tafuna, E. Samoa on Friday, 21st April 1961 (Fiji date: Saturday, 22nd April). Some delegates then proceeded in special flights to Faleolo, W. Samoa and by bus to Malua. Those who remained overnight were entertained by the churches in Pagopago. The 'air lift' from Tafuna was completed on Saturday, 22nd April, and the Conference assembled for its opening session at 7.30 p.m.

PROGRAMME

SATURDAY, 22nd APRIL 1961

7.30 p.m. OPENING SESSION –
     Welcome by the Chairman, Dr. S. Havea.
     Welcome, on behalf of the Churches in Samoa – Pastor Ioelu.
     Introductions.
     Greetings were presented from missionary and other organizations, and from Queen Salote of Tonga.
     Announcements.
     SERVICE OF WORSHIP, conducted by the Chairman, Dr. S. Havea.

SUNDAY, 23rd APRIL 1961

     Delegates visited 38 local congregations, took part in the services and were entertained in the homes of pastors.

MONDAY, 24th APRIL 1961

7.00 a.m. Morning Prayers – conducted by Mr. Stahl Mileng (New Guinea)
     7.30 – Breakfast
8.30 a.m. PLENARY SESSION – Chairman's Address. Dr. S. Havea (Tonga)
     10.15 – Morning Tea
10.45 a.m. PLENARY SESSION – Topic A: 'THE MINISTRY'
     Addresses by the Rev. J. P. Kabel (New Guinea)
                   Bishop Lesslie Newbigin (I.M.C.)
     12.15 – Lunch
     3.30 – Tea
4.00 p.m. PLENARY SESSION – Topic B: 'THE UNFINISHED EVANGELISTIC TASK'
     Addresses by the Rev. Leonard Alafurai (Solomon Islands)
                   the Rev. Hans-Ruedi Weber (W.C.C.)
5.30 p.m. Evening Prayers – conducted by the Rev. Kaitara Metai (Gilbert Islands)

6.00 – Evening Meal

7.30 p.m. EVENING MEETING – the film, 'Men of Two Worlds', illustrating economic and social changes in Fiji, was shown

TUESDAY, 25th APRIL 1961

7.00 a.m. Morning Prayers – conducted by Mr. Stahl Mileng (New Guinea)

7.30 – Breakfast

8.30 a.m. PLENARY SESSION – Bible Study (1) Leader: Rev. H. R. Weber

9.00 a.m. Bible Study in groups. (The Bible Study throughout the Conference was on the Letter to the Galatians)

10.15 – Morning Tea

10.45 a.m. PLENARY SESSION – Topic C: 'THE RELEVANCE OF THE GOSPEL TO THE CHANGING CONDITIONS OF LIFE IN THE PACIFIC'
Addresses by the Rev. B. G. Thorogood (Cook Islands)
the Rev. R. K. Orchard (I.M.C.)

12.15 – Lunch

3.30 – Tea

4.00 p.m. PLENARY SESSION – Topic D: 'THE PLACE OF YOUNG PEOPLE IN THE LIFE OF THE CHURCH'
Addresses by the Rev. Ta Upu Pere (Cook Islands)
U Kyaw Than (E.A.C.C.)

5.30 p.m. Evening Prayers – conducted by the Rev. Kaitara Metai (Gilbert Islands)

6.00 – Evening Meal

7.30 p.m. PLENARY SESSION – Topic E: 'THE CHRISTIAN FAMILY'
Addresses by the Rev. S. Raapoto (Tahiti) (in French)
Mrs. M. G. Wyllie (Australia)

WEDNESDAY, 26th APRIL 1961

7.00 a.m. Morning Prayers – conducted by Mr. Stahl Mileng (New Guinea)

7.30 – Breakfast

8.30 a.m. PLENARY SESSION – Bible Study (2) Leader: Rev. H. R. Weber

9.00 a.m. Bible Study in groups

10.15 – Morning Tea

10.45 a.m. Meetings of five COMMISSIONS (Session 1)

12.15 – Lunch

3.30 – Tea

4.00 p.m. Meetings of five COMMISSIONS (Session 2)

5.30 p.m. Evening Prayers – conducted by the Rev. Kaitara Metai (Gilbert Islands)

         6.00 – Evening Meal

7.30 p.m. EVENING MEETING – 'News of the Pacific Churches' was presented by representatives of the three territories of New Guinea, the Solomon Islands, Fiji and Tonga, in a programme arranged by the Rev. Raymond Perry and the Rev. S. G. C. Cowled

THURSDAY, 27th APRIL 1961

7.00 a.m. Morning Prayers – conducted by Mr. Stahl Mileng (New Guinea)

         7.30 – Breakfast

8.30 a.m. PLENARY SESSION – Bible Study (3) Leader: Rev. H. R. Weber

9.00 a.m. Bible Study in groups

         10.15 – Morning Tea

10.45 a.m. Meetings of five COMMISSIONS (Session 3)

         12.15 – Lunch

         3.30 – Tea

4.00 p.m. Meetings of five COMMISSIONS (Session 4)

5.30 p.m. Evening Prayers – conducted by the Rev. Kaitara Metai (Gilbert Islands)

         6.00 – Evening Meal

7.30 p.m. EVENING MEETING – 'Samoan Cultural Evening', a programme of traditional and contemporary songs and dances, presented by nurses in training and students of Malua College

FRIDAY, 28th APRIL 1961

7.00 a.m. Morning Prayers – conducted by Mr. Stahl Mileng (New Guinea)

         7.30 – Breakfast

8.30 a.m. PLENARY SESSION – Bible Study (4) Leader: Rev. H. R. Weber

9.00 a.m. Bible Study in groups

         10.15 – Morning Tea

10.45 a.m. Meetings of five COMMISSIONS (Session 5)

         12.15 – Lunch

         3.30 – Tea

4.00 p.m. PLENARY SESSION – Discussion on Church Relations in the Pacific and on the Follow-up of the Conference

5.30 p.m. Evening Prayers – conducted by the Rev. Kaitara Metai (Gilbert Islands)

         6.00 – Evening Meal

7.30 p.m. EVENING MEETING – 'News from Churches in other areas', from Asia by U Kyaw Than, from Indonesia by the Rev. Ardi Soejatno, from Europe by the Rev. Hans-Ruedi Weber, from Hawaii by the Rev. J. J. Bevilacqua

SATURDAY, 29th APRIL 1961

The Churches in Samoa invited the delegates to a traditional Kava ceremony at which representatives of the Governments of Eastern and Western Samoa and of the business community were also present.

This was followed by the presentation of gifts from the Churches in Samoa to all members of the Conference, dances by girls of the Avoka and Papauta Schools, and a Samoan feast in traditional style, at the conclusion of which the Conference presented tokens of its gratitude to the Churches in Samoa. The High Commissioner in Western Samoa and Mrs. Wright invited the members of the Conference to a picnic and tea at his residence, and some delegates visited Robert Louis Stevenson's grave at Vailima.

At 7.30 p.m. – Archbishop N. A. Lesser conducted a Service of Preparation for Sunday Worship.

SUNDAY, 30th APRIL 1961

At 8.15 a.m. – the Samoan Church (L.M.S.) and the Congregation at Malua held a Celebration of the Sacrament of the Lord's Supper according to the use of the Church of South India, and invited members of the Conference to join with them. The ministers at this service were Bishop Lesslie Newbigin of the Church of South India, and the Rev. Kenape Faletoese of Malua who preached the sermon on Christian Unity.

Thereafter, members of the Conference visited local congregations and took part in the services.

MONDAY, 1st MAY 1961

7.00 a.m. Morning Prayers – conducted by the Rev. Xowie Madine (New Caledonia) (in French)

7.30 – Breakfast

8.30 a.m. PLENARY SESSION – Bible Study (5) Leader: Rev. H. R. Weber

9.00 a.m. Bible Study in groups

10.15 – Morning Tea

10.45 a.m. PLENARY SESSION – Presentation and consideration of Report from Commission A
(Chairman: Rev. S. A. Tuilovoni (Fiji))

12.15 – Lunch

3.30 – Tea

4.00 p.m. PLENARY SESSION – Presentation and consideration of Report from Commission B
(Chairman: Rev. L. D. Fullerton (Fiji))

5.30 p.m. Evening Prayers – conducted by Archbishop N. A. Lesser (New Zealand)

6.00 – Evening Meal

7.30 p.m. EVENING MEETING – 'News of the Pacific Churches' was presented by representatives from the New Hebrides, New Caledonia and Tahiti, and from the Marshall, Caroline, Cook, Gilbert and Ellice Islands, Niue and Nauru, in a programme arranged by M. le pasteur H. Vernier and Dr. Harold Hanlin

TUESDAY, 2nd MAY, 1961

7.00 a.m. Morning Prayers – conducted by the Rev. Xowie Madine (New Caledonia) (in French)

7.30 – Breakfast

8.30 a.m. PLENARY SESSION – Bible Study (6) Leader: Rev. H. R. Weber

9.00 a.m. Bible Study in groups

10.15 – Morning Tea

10.45 a.m. PLENARY SESSION – Presentation and consideration of Report from Commission C
(Chairman: Rev. A. G. Horwell (New Hebrides))

12.15 – Lunch

3.30 – Tea

3.45 p.m. PLENARY SESSION – Continuation of Discussion of Church Relations in the Pacific and on the Follow-up of the Conference

5.30 p.m. Evening Prayers – conducted by Archbishop N. A. Lesser (New Zealand)

6.00 – Evening Meal

7.30 p.m. PLENARY SESSION – Presentation and consideration of Report from Commission D
(Chairman: Rev. J. T. Tamahori (New Zealand))

WEDNESDAY, 3rd MAY 1961

7.00 a.m. Morning Prayers – conducted by the Rev. Xowie Madine (New Caledonia) (in French)

7.30 – Breakfast

8.30 a.m. PLENARY SESSION – Bible Study (7) Leader: Rev. H. R. Weber

9.00 a.m. Bible Study in groups

10.15 – Morning Tea

10.45 a.m. PLENARY SESSION – Presentation and consideration of Report from Commission E (Chairman: Mrs. Fetaui Mataafa (Samoa))

12.15 – Lunch

3.30 – Tea

4.00 p.m. PLENARY SESSION – Business arising from Commission Reports and discussion of Follow-up of the Conference

5.30 p.m. Evening Prayers – conducted by Archbishop N. A. Lesser (New Zealand)

6.00 – Evening Meal

7.30 p.m. EVENING MEETING – 'News Session'; news of the I.M.C. (Bishop Lesslie Newbigin), W.C.C. (Rev. Hans-Ruedi Weber), E.A.C.C. (U Kyaw Than), from the Torres Straits (Rev. Boggo Pilot) and from Africa (Rev. R. K. Orchard), and information about the Pacific Literature Society (Rev. J. M. Stuckey).

THURSDAY, 4th MAY 1961

7.00 a.m. Morning Prayers – conducted by the Rev. Xowie Madine (New Caledonia) (in French)

7.30 – Breakfast

8.30 a.m. PLENARY SESSION – Bible Study (8) Leader: Rev. H. R. Weber

9.00 a.m. Bible Study in groups

10.15 – Morning Tea

10.45 a.m. CLOSING SESSION – Unfinished Business, and Expressions of Appreciation

11.00 a.m. CONCLUDING SERVICE OF WORSHIP – conducted by the Chairman; the Sermon preached by Bishop Lesslie Newbigin

The Continuation Committee appointed during the Conference met during the afternoon and evening of Thursday, 4th May. The 'air lift' of Conference members to Tafuna, E. Samoa began during the afternoon of Thursday, 4th May and continued during the morning of Friday, 5th May. The majority of members proceeded by the special flight from Tafuna at 3.0 p.m. on Friday, 5th May, arriving in Nadi, Fiji at 5.0 p.m. on Saturday, 6th May (Fiji date). Many of them remained in Fiji for the Consultation on Theological Education held by the Theological Education Fund of the I.M.C. in Suva from 8th – 13th May 1961.

Commissions on Topics

Chairmen

A (The Ministry) — Rev. S. A. Tuilovoni (Fiji)
B (Unfinished Task of Evangelism) — Rev. L. D. Fullerton (Fiji)
C (Relevance of Gospel to Changing Conditions) — Rev. A. G. Horwell (New Hebrides)
D (Young People) — Rev. J. T. Tamahori (New Zealand)
E (Christian Family) — Mrs. Fetaui Mataafa (Samoa)

Bible Groups

Leaders

1 Dr. A. C. Frerichs (New Guinea)
2 Rev. Mila Sapolu (Samoa)
3 Rev. John Heine (Marshall Is.)
4 Bishop J. C. Vockler (Australia)
5 Rev. Marc-André Ledoux (New Caledonia)
6 Rev. K. B. Osborne (New Guinea)
7 Mr. Enosi Bailoloi (New Guinea)

The Ministry

Address by Rev. J. P. Kabel (New Guinea)

The Ministry of the Church

It is a wonderful experience to meet each other here at Samoa, after having worked separately during so many years.

We received some information about one another, and we discovered that all over the area we are wrestling with the same problems.

It is a good thing, therefore, that we have this opportunity to meet in order to speak about our experiences in the past, our problems of the present, our hopes and our plans for the future.

The central question seems to direct our attention to the past, and the results of the past seen in the present time. This question is defined as follows: "How far has the Gospel become the controlling fact in the life of our churches?".

But the sub-topics immediately direct our attention to the problems of the present—a general attitude of scepticism and secularism, new sects grasping the opportunity defined as "a vacuum created at the centre of the spiritual life".

And for the future, we have to learn that the Church should be the place where the power of the Holy Spirit is given to men to enable them to live lives of joy and victory over sin.

I think that it needs no explanation why the ministry of the Church is one of the sub-topics. We have to study the question how the Church *is* equipped, and how the Church *should be* equipped. The latter question is not merely a question of practice and efficiency. We think about the question how the Church should be equipped; that means that we are speaking about a theological question.

It is, of course, very important how the churches in our area *are* equipped at this moment. It would be most interesting to see how the various theological principles have been adapted to the specific needs and possibilities of the various regions.

But the present address would offer more than a mere historic survey. Our purpose is to look for the meaning of the ministry of the Church.

I think we have to pay attention to three main points:

    A. The Biblical doctrine of the ministry.

    B. The problems raised by the old religious and social structure.

    C. Our conclusions for the actual situation.

A. *The Biblical Doctrine of the Ministry.*

We are together in this Conference as representatives of widely different theological traditions. This fact can neither be denied nor neglected. But at the same time we confess our unity in the crucified and risen Lord. Not our traditions, but the will of our Lord should be decisive for our churches and the forms of their service and witness in the world.

We have to listen together to the witness of the Scripture. We shall not find there a complete set of instructions concerning organiza- tion, but we certainly shall find the necessary directives for the Church, how it has to serve and to witness in the world until the Lord comes.

When we are studying the Scriptures with an eye to the Church and its ministry, we certainly cannot restrict ourselves to the New Testa- ment. The "roots" of the New Testament teaching are to be sought in the Old Testament. To understand the ministry of the Church, we have to look at the Old Testament doctrine about the Covenant. In teaching this central subject, two aspects are stressed. On one hand great stress is laid upon the Holiness of God. He does not need man. On the other hand, this Holy God loves man and makes His Covenant with him.

Fundamental is the choosing and calling act of God. The act of man is a reaction, an answer.

The Old Testament, therefore, likes to use the word "servant". This word is used for special persons, e.g. Moses and Abraham, but it is also used for the "special" ministers of the covenant: the prophets, the priests and the kings. In a well-known Old Testament theology (W. Eichrodt: *Theologie des Alten Testamentes*) these ministers are called the organs of the covenant. They have a most important role among the people of God, but they are organs of the covenant, the expression of the relation between God and His chosen people. The people itself may also be called "servant". This is expressed in the well-known passage Exodus 19:1-6, although the term "servant" is not used here. We find the term in the well-known Songs of the Suffering Servant (e.g. Jer. 49:3). But in the same songs, the ultimate remnant, the person of one, suffering and dying for the sins of others, comes to us as "the Servant of the Lord".

All these lines meet in Jesus Christ. He is the mediator of the New Covenant, a covenant in His Blood (Luke 22:20).

The ministry of this new covenant is the ministry of reconciliation: "And all things are of God, who hath reconciled us to himself by Jesus Christ, and hath given to us the ministry of reconciliation". (2 Cor. 5:18.)

Most important for the understanding of the ministry of the Church is Ephesians 4:11, 12, which reads in the King James Version: "And he gave some apostles; and some prophets; and some evangelists; and some pastors and teachers; for the perfecting of the saints, for the work of the ministry, for the edifying of the body of Christ". This translation gives the impression that three things are parallel: perfecting the saints, work of the ministry, edifying the body of Christ.

Luther translates in another way, and also the so-called Zwingli Bible. In this translation the second part of the text reads as follows: "in order to equip the saints for the work of the ministry, for the edifying of the Body of Christ".

Apostles, prophets, evangelists, pastors and teachers, our "special" ministers, have to equip the saints for the work of the ministry.

The work of the ministry, according to this text, is *not* the work of a small, specialised group, but the work of all the saints of the whole Church.

This should be related to Paul's teaching about the "ministry of reconciliation". It is clear that God reconciles by Jesus Christ ; that means the essential ministry in the Church is the ministry of the Risen and Ever-Present Lord Himself. This ministry is given to us, the Church, the Body of Christ, and it is the task of those whom we call ministers to equip the whole Church for the work of this ministry.

From one centre, two lines are developed in New Testament teaching: the priesthood of all believers (I Peter 2:9, 10), and the specialised ministry.

How these lines are linked we saw above. It might be necessary to stress that these two lines never can be separated. The specialised or settled ministry cannot be loosened from the priesthood of all believers. The specialised ministry has *no* purpose in itself, but aims at the perfecting of all the saints in the above-mentioned sense.

Besides that, the specialised ministry cannot be loosened from the ministry of the Lord Himself. Both the so-called laity and the so-called ministry take part in the ministry of the Lord Himself. Before the Lord, all members of the Church are laymen. The *laici,* the laymen, are those who belong to the *laos,* that is the People of God.

The ministry of the Lord Himself is usually described as a three-fold ministry. His ministry is priestly, kingly and prophetic.

This well-known scheme can be very helpful in understanding the character and purpose of Christ's work, and therefore also of the work of the ministry:

As a priest, Christ sacrifices Himself.

As a king, He realises the kingdom of God.

As a prophet, He reveals the reality of the reconciliation worked by Him as the Lord who, priestly, became Servant, and as the Servant who, in a kingly way, became Lord.

In this ministry the whole Body of Christ takes part. And it is the task of the specialised ministry to assist the members of the Body to realise this partaking.

B. *The Problems raised by the Old Religious and Social Structure.*

Before drawing some practical conclusions, we must look now at the problems raised by the old structure.

In that old structure we also find priestly, kingly, and prophetic aspects. In a comparative study of religion the holy persons are described under the headings Prophet, Priest and King (cf. The Studies of Dr. G. v. D. Leeuw, and Prof. Dr. Th. van Baaren: *"Wy-mensen").* We find these aspects in the old religion of our area too. There are heathen prophets, priests, and kings. Their function must be understood from the point of view of heathen thinking.

In his religion the heathen looks for well-being (in which salvation is included), social, physical and spiritual. He looks for the realization of it and he is trying to keep it under his control.

But man is always in the centre of all things. He looks for well-being. He is trying to realize it in the ordinary way, performing the rites prescribed by the ancestors; or in the extraordinary way, e.g. by cargo cults. And it is again man himself who tries to keep control by clinging to the inherited way of life.

It is the heathen prophet who is searching after the secrets of the hidden world. He has to know the means to make contact with that other world. But the secret is always a hidden secret: it is the deceptive secret, the secret of the serpent that beguiled.

Here we meet with a real danger for the ministry. Our ministry, the ministry of the Church and the specialized ministry, can never be prophetic in this sense. We are not searching after a secret of well-being. Christianity does not offer a system of religious knowledge necessary for this well-being.

This kind of prophetism leads to sects, with all kinds of special beliefs and special behaviour necessary for salvation. Or it leads to a totally secularised building up of a new world; social improvement becomes the great slogan then.

In our area, both dangers are very real. Many Christians become adherents of sects because Christianity did not offer what they longed for. Others dedicate themselves to social improvement, and they are prepared to send their children to any kind of school: secular, Roman Catholic or any other.

But the prophetic ministry of the Church has to resist the temptations of heathenism. There is *no* secret to search for; we have to preach the reality of reconciliation. We have to open our lives to the reality of God's Love and to the work of His Spirit.

It is the heathen priest who has to preserve and safeguard the sacred traditions. The priest has the know-how; he is leading the cult and performing the rites. Here is the temptation of unspiritual conservatism, of a clinging to traditional forms. The legalism of Judaism is a good example of this temptation. Therefore the letter of Paul to the Galatians, in which Paul struggles with this legalism, is so very important for us in our situation.

A priestly ministry of this kind lays too much stress upon forms and traditions. There is no openness for the spiritual and physical needs of the flock. A certain pattern of life is maintained. The statement of the advisory group says: "Our churches often seem to be more governed by fear than by love, more concerned to enforce conformity to certain laws of behaviour than to show their love to God by loving and forgiving others". We must see clearly that this is a result of a heathen understanding of priestly work.

The priestly ministry, too, has to resist the temptations of heathenism. We cannot be priests who maintain certain forms of life and worship. Our priestly ministry is the ministry of Christ, who sacrificed Himself. Our task is *not* to tie and to hold, but to let go. Our priestly ministry has to realise the reconciliation worked by Christ.

The meaning of this reconciliation, of the victory of Christ, has to be shown in our private lives, in the lives of our congregations, and in our society. Our lives may be full of hope, full of signs of renewal.

It is the heathen king who represents god-on-earth. In him eternal life is present and through him the community shares the blessings of the cosmic order. It is true that kings are found only in a part of the Pacific. But among our people we find kingly figures in the mythology. People long for a Lord, whose coming will be the beginning of a new golden age.

Around these "Lords" we find the cargo-cults or Messianic movements. Here we find a longing for glorification of the personal life, the life of the nation, or of the tribe. Here the cross becomes a stumbling block. The glory of these Messianic Lords is the glory of his nation and the glory of his special servants!

But a crucified Messiah asks for humble, self-denying service. The glory and the honour of the nations has to be brought into the heavenly city.

The kingly ministry is a ministry of self-denying love and service. The Church cannot seek honour and glory for itself, and has to be careful and critical concerning national honour and national glory. This perhaps will be very acute in the coming years.

C. *Our Conclusions for the Actual Situation.*

The problems we have in the actual situation in our area are the result of the old ways of thinking and believing, often continued in a Christian dress, and by the influence of the New Age, the coming of the Great Society and all the rapid changes caused by it.

In the second part of this address we looked at some of the old ways of thinking.

Now we have to say something about the special difficulties of modern times. Dr. Hoekendyk has a short but most important chapter in his doctoral thesis about the Great Society. In this chapter he shows that the problem is a world-wide problem, and not only a problem caused by the meeting of Western and Eastern cultures. The Great Society is characterised by him as economic, secular and collectivistic, while the old culture was communal, sacral, and with a traditional structure. There is no possibility of preserving the old way of life. The Church should not pay attention only to groups which still maintain the traditional way of life, but also to those who have loosened from the old structure.

Nationalism cannot give a definite solution to these problems.

In his last chapter, "Comprehensive approach", Dr. Hoekendyk gives three general directives:

(a) The congregation as a whole has to work in the task of evangelisation, and in the translation of its message into practical service.

(b) The congregation has to direct its services to all parts of life at the same time.

(c) In its service the congregation has to become a centre of social integration, in giving an example of ordered life.

I think that Dr. Hoekendyk gives a most important programme in this short outline. It is clearly shown that it is *not* our task to preserve the old order of things. In the new circumstances, the Church is not allowed to weep about the past, but has to fulfil its ministry under the present circumstances.

Most important, too, is Dr. Hoekendyk's stress upon the task of the whole congregation, as a centre of witness and service. This fits with our findings about Biblical doctrine.

That the congregation has to direct its service to *all* parts of life has to be repeated over and over again. In our area, most of the people look on the Church as a department for the salvation of souls. It is not easy to open their eyes to the comprehensive task of the Church. During the elections for the New Guinea Council at the beginning of this year, this again became very clear.

There is no room to elaborate these points. We must come to some practical conclusions concerning the ministry.

In the first place, the whole Church, the whole congregation must be in the centre of our thinking and planning. We are not allowed to pick out of the laity some able men and women to enlarge the clergy with a kind of semi-clergy. The task of the specialized ministers is the preparation of all the saints for their ministry, for their special part in the edifying of the Body of Christ.

The training of our ministers has to be directed to this. In their teaching in Bible classes and confirmation classes, and also in their preaching work, our ministers have to guide all the members to maturity (see the Moffat translation of Eph. 4:3).

In their training, "the edifying of the Body" should be central. Special attention should be paid to pastoral care. Personal contact with the members of the congregation is most important. This has to be taught theoretically and practically. Better trained ministers should not become church managers. Further, our ministers need thorough theoretical knowledge to get a clear insight into the nature of the Church and its service and the nature of modern man and his needs. The theological school is defined by Professor Niebuhr as "the intellectual centre of the Church's life". (*The purpose of the Church and its Ministry*—in the section: "The Character and Purpose of a Theological School".)

The ministers themselves must understand what is asked from the whole Church, in order to help the Church to witness and to serve in the actual situation. Therefore they need also training in cultural anthropology and sociology to understand the growth of nationalism, resurgence of ancient beliefs and the attractive power of sects.

Surely an intellectual insight is not sufficient. One may have a perfect understanding, without drawing the right conclusions or without finding the right behaviour. Intellectual truth always has to be related to Christian ethics. The minister has to fulfil the great commandment to love God, not only with his mind, but first of all with all his heart, that is, with the centre of the totality of his life.

Together with the whole Church, which they help to fulfil its ministry, the ministers themselves have to be built upon the foundation of which Christ Himself is the chief corner stone, "in whom *all* the building, fitly framed together, groweth unto an holy temple in the Lord".

The Ministry

Address by Consultant, Bishop Lesslie Newbigin
(International Missionary Council)

As one who has no previous knowledge of the Pacific area I cannot pretend to say anything about the special tasks of the ministry in the Pacific island churches at this time. I shall do no more than meditate with you on certain passages of Scripture which speak to the Church everywhere concerning the ministry. May I also say that in this talk I shall use the words "Pastor" and "Minister" indiscriminately to refer to those who are ordained to the ministry of word, sacraments, and pastoral care.

I

I begin with St. John, chapter 13, which is surely the essential starting point for all thinking about Christian ministry. St. John introduces with special solemnity his description of Jesus' washing of the disciples' feet. It was, he says, a moment when Jesus knew "that the Father had given all things into His hands, and that He had come from God and was going to God". It was as one filled with the full consciousness of His divine authority that He stooped down to do the work of a servant, and thereby to gather into one deed the revelation of God which He had come to make.

This is something utterly shocking to all our established ideas of authority. It turns everything upside down. We can surely sympathise with Peter's indignant words: "What, Lord? *You*, wash *my* feet? Never". We are all glad to do service to those whom we recognise to be above us, with the understanding that we can expect to receive service from those whom we consider to be below us. There is not one of us who would not count it a supreme honour to be allowed to wash the feet of Jesus; we might even compete with each other for the position. But that is not what He asks of us; He requires us to permit Him to wash our feet. And this means a revolution, an overturning of all established order. We must take seriously the words which the Lord addresses to Peter: "What I am doing you do not know now; you will understand afterwards". It is impossible for Peter to understand it until he has been through the experience of the Cross and the Resurrection, until he has been through the death and rebirth which Christ came to make possible. This is not just a bit of moral instruction, a vivid lesson in humility. It is the prefiguring of that total revolution which was to be accomplished in the Cross.

When the Lord had washed their feet, He resumed his garments, and His place at their head. He *is* master and Lord; let there be no mistake about this. And this is what lordship is; all else is counterfeit. The consequence is obvious. "If I, your Lord and Teacher, have washed your feet, you also ought to wash one another's feet." There is no escape from that. A servant is not greater than his Lord. And this has a very special application. An apostle (for that is the word hidden behind the English translation "He that is sent") is not greater than He who made him an apostle. If we are to think about the apostolic ministry, there is where we must start.

There is, alas, a long and sad story which could be told of the Church's forgetfulness of this word, of the attempt—often successful —by the ministers of the Church to exercise the kind of authority which Jesus refused to exercise. We do not need to go back to the prince-bishops of mediaeval Europe for examples. There have been times in India—and perhaps elsewhere—when the district missionary and his Indian successor exercised a kind of authority over the Christians in his district which is certainly not the authority manifested in this chapter. I was recently reading a study of Ghana by a person who is both psychiatrist and anthropologist. The book contained numerous case-records, and it struck me in reading them that these African villagers when referring to the local Christian minister always called him "The Rev. Manager". That is the image of the Christian ministry which we have somehow managed to present.

What is distressing is to see how surprised Christians are when a Christian minister acts in the way which is here laid down. A brother-bishop in the Church of South India was faced by a dissident movement in his diocese. Its leader openly and persistently flouted his authority and tried to humiliate him. The bishop refused to react otherwise than by humbly accepting insult, and seeking a change of heart. One day the dissident leader announced that he was ready to make peace and to hand over the key of the house which he was holding in defiance of the decision of the Church. Quite a meeting gathered for the occasion. But when it came to the point, the man announced that he had changed his mind, and instead of handing over the key, publicly humiliated the bishop again. People were astonished when the bishop refused to retaliate in any way, but quietly spoke to the man and left. To-day there is a unity in that diocese which could never have come if the bishop had tried to exercise a worldly authority. But why is it that Christians are astonished when a bishop behaves as Christ told us to behave, and remembers that "a servant is not greater than his master"?

St. Paul has told us, in an unforgettable passage, that the Son of God emptied himself and took the form of a servant. The first thing to be said about the Christian ministry is that it must be conformed to that pattern.

II

I turn now to another passage in which our Lord speaks about the nature of this ministry. In St. Luke 12:35 ff, we find the warning that the Master's servants must be alert, with loins girt and lamps burning, like men who wait for their Lord. When Peter asks: "Lord, are you telling this parable for us or for all?", Jesus answers: "Who then is the faithful and wise steward whom his master will set over his household to give them their portion of food at the proper time?". Here there is a further definition of the kind of service which ministers are to give: they are stewards.

Of course all Christ's people are stewards. St. Peter tells us that each of us is to employ the gifts he has received for one another "as good stewards of God's varied grace" (I Peter 4:10). God's gifts are infinitely varied, and every Christian has a stewardship in respect of the gifts with which he has been entrusted. What, then, are the special gifts which are entrusted to those who are ordained to what we call the Holy Ministry? There would probably be differences among us in answering this question, differences which it would be useful to talk over in the Commission on the Ministry. But in general we should probably all agree that they are entrusted with a stewardship in respect of Word, Sacraments, and Pastoral Care. Let us look for a moment at each of these.

a. *The Ministry of the Word.* Every ordained minister is ordained to a stewardship in respect of the Word of God. Christ, who is Himself the Word of God, makes Himself present to His people as the means of their life by the word faithfully read and explained in a language which the people understand. The minister is entrusted with the infinitely solemn responsibility of being the means by which this happens. He does not stand before the congregation to put forward his own ideas, but to be the means by which the word of God is spoken. It is a great comfort to me whenever I stand in the pulpit, to see that the Bible is in front of me, between me and the people, and to remember that my reason for being there is simply to be the means which the Holy Spirit may use to make the words of this Book become the living word of God to them. I have been trained for the ministry in a church which does not use a fixed lectionary, and in which it is left to the minister to decide each Sunday what lessons he will read and on what subject he will preach. Since coming into a united church I have had to minister to many congregations which use a set lectionary. I have therefore had to learn to accept lessons which I would not myself have chosen on that particular day. Often, as I have prepared to preach, I have wished that I could have almost any other text, because it seemed that the given passage was quite useless. But I have learned that when I wrestle with the given passage until I find the Word of God in it, I have had over and over again the experience that it was precisely this word which was needed for the congregation. I have begun to learn in a new way what a wonderful thing is this stewardship of the word of God, and how—if the steward is even a little faithful—God enables him to bring constantly new treasures out of His word for the strengthening of His household.

b. *The Ministry of the Sacraments.* Those who are ordained as ministers are also given a stewardship of the sacraments—those enacted words of God by which He incorporates us into His Church and continually renews our communion with Him. These sacraments are not ours to do as we like with. They belong to the Master of the house, and they are entrusted to the stewards to be dispensed according to His will. If we understand this, we shall understand how much care and thought must go into the preparation both of minister and people for the acts of the sacraments, and with what reverence and care everything connected with them should be done.

c. *Pastoral Care.* This is not, of course, the concern of ordained ministers alone. There is a sense in which we are all responsible for the pastoral care of one another. All the members of the household of God should be seeking to build one another up in love, according to their different gifts. But those who are ordained to the holy ministry are given a special responsibility in this regard. They are to be pastors of the flock of Christ. This is a unique office for which there is really no equivalent in non-Christian society. For this reason it is often misunderstood and neglected, especially in strongly pagan societies. It is also difficult work, costly in time and spiritual resources. For this reason it is often neglected in favour of work which demands less, and seems to produce more. I do not want to speak much of it except to say this: I believe that the simplest test to apply to any pastoral work is to ask yourself: "Do I pray regularly, by name, for every person for whom I have any pastoral responsibility?". I believe that the centre of true pastoral work is there, and that if this work is truly and faithfully done, the rest will flow from it.

The minister is thus a steward on behalf of God's household in respect of Word, Sacraments, and Pastoral care. Is this too obvious to need repeating? I do not think so. I can think of situations where it seems that ministers are urged and expected to do almost everything except these three things. One of my fellow-bishops in the Church of South India has spoken of the "fatal *ad*" which we put before "minister" so that we become more interested in administration than in ministering. Doubtless there are many other things

which ministers must do from time to time for the good of the household of God. But they ought not to push out of the central place
these three things in which ministers are entrusted with a stewardship.

III

I turn now to look briefly at another passage which speaks of the
minister as a watchman (Ezekiel 33 : 1-7). The watchman is set by
God to give warning to the city when danger approaches. The
prophet is told that he has been appointed to this task. The same
thought is applied to ministers of the Church where it is said in the
Epistle to the Hebrews (13 : 17): "Obey your leaders and submit to
them ; for they are keeping watch over your souls as men who will
have to give an account. Let them do this joyfully and not sadly,
for that would be of no advantage to you".

The watchman's task is a lonely one. He must stand on the wall or
on the watchtower when other people are in their homes or mingling
in the ordinary life of the street and the market-place. And he must
not expect to be popular. We are familiar with the kind of difficulties
he faces. If an ordinary member of the congregation is going astray,
a small man who does not have much influence in the community,
it will not be very difficult to warn him. If a powerful man, the chief
man of the village, the biggest contributor to the church funds, is
going astray, it is more difficult. The pastor is tempted to keep quiet
for the sake of peace. He knows that if he earns the hostility of the
big man, there may be much trouble for the flock. But if he is a
true pastor he will blow the trumpet and give warning, facing whatever consequences may come.

To be a true watchman he must be a man who is not afraid to
stand alone, who is ready to spend long vigils alone with God, listening for His word. He must be a man who knows what it is to be
alone with God, and for whom the voice of God is not being drowned
by the clamour of other voices.

IV

And lastly I want to speak about a text of scripture on which Mr.
Kabel has already spoken—Ephesians 4 : 12. This text is very important for our understanding of the relation between the special work
of the "holy ministry", and the general ministry in which all Christian
people share. According to this verse the special ministries were
given "to equip the saints for the work of ministering, for building up
the body of Christ". In most of the English translations a comma
has been wrongly inserted after "saints", which makes it appear that
the ministry is given to equip the saints *and* for the work of ministering. This mis-translation reflects all too clearly the wrong conception
of the ministry which has become so common in the churches, according to which the ministry of the *whole* body has been forgotten and
ministry has been regarded as the task of a small professional class.
The Biblical understanding of the matter is not so. According to the

Bible, all Christ's people are called to share in a common ministry. They are all part of the royal priesthood which Christ has ordained to represent Him in the world. They are called to take their part in representing to the world His kingly rule and His priestly service on behalf of all men. The special ministries which are listed in verse 11 are provided to equip the people of God for the fulfilment of this general ministry.

As the royal priesthood on earth, the Church has a double task in relation to the world. It must represent God before men by its preaching and its loving service, being in all its words and works a means of bringing God's holy love to men. And at the same time it must represent men before God, offering up on behalf of all men the prayers they cannot offer, bearing on behalf of all men the guilt they cannot accept. Both sides of this double ministry are the work of the whole body. It is the whole body which must set forth the Gospel and reveal the love of God in action. It is the whole body which offers up prayers and sacrifices. In every liturgy of Christendom, when the great eucharistic prayer is offered in the Holy Communion, even though it is said by a single minister it is always said in the first person plural. It is the whole royal priesthood which is in action.

But within the royal priesthood there is a special ministry of those who are called to the stewardship of word and sacraments and pastoral care. Their work is to be to the Church what the Church is to be to the world. They are the servants of the servants of God, the priests of the priests of God, the evangelists of the heralds of God. They are entrusted with the stewardship of those gifts of the risen Lord by which the Church is constantly renewed in its royal and priestly character.

The test, therefore, of a minister's work is not to be found in the number and quality of the things that he does, or that he gets the Church to do. It is to be found in the way in which the lay members of his congregation carry on their secular life in the world, in the degree to which all their daily life from Monday to Saturday is part of the royal priesthood of Christ on behalf of all men. The test is whether or not he is "equipping the saints for the work of ministry".

In this as in all else, the basis and pattern of the work of the ministry is to be found in the work of the great High Priest Himself. One sees this pattern with a special clarity in that wonderful prayer which is often called the High Priestly prayer, or the Prayer of Consecration. If there were time it would be good to study the whole of this prayer, (St. John 17), but let me pick out only three verses.

In verse 6, the Lord says of His disciples that God has given them to Him "out of the world" and that to them He has "manifested the Name" of God. They have been brought out of the world and given to Jesus, in order that they might receive the revelation of God's nature and the impress of His character. But then in verse 18 we see that they have been brought out of the world in order to be sent into the world, just as Jesus Himself was sent into the world.

And in verse 19 He says: "And for their sake I consecrate myself, that they also may be consecrated in truth".

The minister's consecration is based upon and patterned upon that consecration. It is in order that those whom God has given him may be consecrated in truth and sent into the world as the concrete manifestation of the name and nature and glory of God in the midst of the secular life of the world.

The corruption of the ministry occurs when it is seen as a position of authority for the organising and controlling of men for the purpose of carrying out some programme. The glory of the Christian ministry is seen in the lives of Christian laymen and women in the world. When Christian men and women are truly living as Christians in the midst of the secular world as part of Christ's royal priesthood, then they know that they need precisely that ministry of word and sacraments and pastoral care by which their participation in the royal priesthood is continually renewed. Thus a true ministry and a true laity belong together.

The Unfinished Evangelistic Task

Address by Rev. Leonard Alafurai (Solomon Islands)

It is an honour and privilege, not to me only, but also to my Church in Melanesia, to be asked to present to this Conference an address on this subject. My only regret is that it is I that should be asked to address the Conference on such an important topic as this.

The unfinished task of proclaiming the Good News is one of the great issues confronting the Church throughout the world to-day. This Unfinished Task of Evangelisation is a true factor when we come to realize the fact that the Church exists in history and that history is the scene of continuous change.

The Bible teaches that history is the sphere and medium in and through which God has chosen to carry out His purpose for the world. We therefore, as members of the Church, are called upon to take a hand in the fulfilment of the purposes of God for the world. It will help us therefore, in this field of our work, to come to some understanding in this Conference of the conditions under which those purposes are coming to fruition ; at the present time the task of the Church in Evangelisation is an Unfinished Task, and it always will be.

At every stage in the proclaiming of the Good News we must review our methods and results, by asking ourselves the following questions: "What have we done?" "What are we going to do?" and "How it is going to be done?". This is the responsibility of every Christian, but before it can be carried out effectively those of us whose responsibility it is to carry the Good News must be alive to the problems of our people. Bishop Selwyn once described the Ministry in Melanesia as "a Black Net with White Corks". And to-day we are realizing the wisdom of these words.

What is Evangelism?

The word as it is used in the Bible means the bringing or the proclaiming of good tidings to one. The early Christian Church in their preaching, however, used the word to mean something more than just a message to a person. To them it was the good tidings of the Kingdom of God and salvation for the whole world through Christ. God came down in the form of man to save all mankind. Our Lord left this Good News in the hands of the early Christian Church with its quickly formulated doctrines and Scriptures to safeguard it from heresy. Our Lord not only left this Good News in the hands of the Church, but also commanded that the Good News should be taken and preached to all the world for the salvation of all mankind. Our Lord said: "There are other sheep I have which are not of this fold: them also I must bring, and they shall hear my voice: and there shall be one fold, and one shepherd".

Christ came and fulfilled all cultures and all people. "A full, perfect and sufficient sacrifice and oblation and satisfaction for the sins of the whole world." Christ Himself said: "I came not to destroy, but to fulfil". Therefore Christ fulfilled the laws of the Old Testament and in the same way he fulfils all other cultures. The Good News is therefore for all mankind—high and low; rich and poor; black and white; red and yellow. But there are some who say: "Why disturb a non-Christian God-conscious society?". But those who ask this type of question do not stop to see or hear the consequences of Western culture on other ethnic groups without Christianity, on Godless nations who have not the love of God before them; this is challenging the Church in the Pacific to-day. We must step in now and fulfil Christ's command. We are all aware of the cargo cults which from time to time have sprung up in different territories throughout the Pacific. What is the cause of this? The failure in this sphere is not due to the insufficiency of the Good News, but largely because it has not been properly given.

To Whom it is to be given

Christ fulfils all cultures. In considering the giving of the Good News, it is not only essential to understand what is the Good News, but also to know those to whom the message is being given. Our Lord said: "I know my sheep" and he adds: "I am known of mine". There must be a mutual understanding between the preacher and the hearer of the Good News before it can be effectively given and readily accepted. Evangelism, as we all know, is not walking into a heathen village waving the Bible, but the heathen must be approached on their own level. Firstly then, effort must be made to understand the culture of the people because if you are to make a strong Church, you must build on the culture of the people and make it their own faith and not Western ideas forced upon them. This is by no means an easy task, and much pruning and reinterpretation is needed to suit the circumstances under which it is to be given. But failure to do this leaves a people who are still heathen, although nominally Christian.

How it is to be given

In Melanesia, apart from Honiara, they are either heathen or Christian. It must be realized that the method I will describe has been used in Melanesia to deal with the particular situation, but I feel that in principle this method with adaptation would be suitable for evangelism in other cultural and religious groups.

We are all aware of the fact that all effective evangelism must have as its basis a prayerful Church, realizing its responsibility towards the heathen or the lapsed. In Melanesia we have in nearly all Christian villages a group of men and women called "Companions". Their work is to pray morning and night for the work of the Church among the heathen. This does not mean that those who are not in this group are not expected to pray for the work, because in our prayer book there is a Prayer provided for the rest of the people in the village to be said when they attend morning and evening prayer. In Melanesia many have been brought to Christianity either directly through the work of the Brotherhood or indirectly through education or medical work. Is this the wrong motive? Father Kelly of the Society of the Sacred Mission once said: "One should never judge a person's motives as they are generally bad". Why are *you* a Christian? Because your parents were Christians? That in itself is surely not the right motive, so you and I cannot be judged by our motives, but what we must do with those we approach is to make their motive, whether good or bad, into something "Good", through giving them a real understanding of the faith.

The work of the Brotherhood is confined mainly to the heathen areas of Melanesia. On entering a village, the first thing that they do is to gain the confidence of the people and then get to understand them by eating, sleeping and living with them and by taking part in their daily activities. In some villages this may be easy and in others it may be difficult. But once a village is converted, the priest of the district is approached to find a catechist to take over from the Brothers who must go on to other heathen areas. The newly converted people are then instructed and catechised either by the priest or the catechist, in preparation for baptism. Thereafter, every Christian should feel morally responsible for the restoring of the lapsed. We often feel that once a man is baptised and confirmed that the task is completed. There must always be a follow-up at all stages in the evangelistic field of our work, not only by the minister but also by the laity.

While stressing the importance of lay evangelism, I feel sure that it must be grounded on a firmly organised evangelistical programme ordered by the Church itself. I believe that the best method must be both corporate and individual. In Melanesia, most of the heathen have been converted and only small pockets of heathen remain on one or two of the main islands. This work has been done as already stated, by the Melanesian Brotherhood. Now, the Melanesian Brotherhood are not only looking further afield to places like New Guinea, but also back to those who they have converted over the last hundred years who have fallen away or become weak. From this you will see that the Brotherhood is in process of change, into becoming a band not only of converters of the heathen but also of lay evangelists who will conduct missions among the converted to strengthen and build the prayer life of the villages. This will have to be carefully organized, just as the method of the conversion of the heathen was the consequence of much forethought. After this, and I believe only after this, can individual evangelism become really effective.

The lay evangelism of the corporate and organized Church must be the foundation of evangelism by the individual laity. The Diocese of Melanesia is divided first into Archdeaconaries of which there are two—the Southern and the Northern Archdeaconaries. These are again divided into Rural Deaneries and there are six of these. These Rural Deaneries are again divided into Districts, which consist of so many villages with a priest in charge. In each village there is placed a catechist who is responsible for the spiritual life of the village by taking morning and evening prayers and reading to them the Word of God day by day. Throughout the Diocese, most of these catechists have had some training in evangelistic work in our Catechist Schools, of which there are three. This briefly is the method we use in Melanesia in our evangelistic task. As we can see from this, this is not a one-man work.

In conclusion, I would like to add that I do not think that in the past there has been enough working together and this has been largely due to the fact that it is felt that doctrinal issues are to be dealt with first and this in itself would make any move toward partnership most involved and difficult. But there are issues which arise where the churches should be united in voice and aim, e.g. education and medical work. A missionary Church becomes involved in many of the so-called secular works and in these no matters of doctrine are involved. All should have in common the desire to save and help the whole man, body, mind and soul, and it is here, I believe, that we should start our working together. In the religious sphere, understanding of differences and sympathy must be the foundation and from this could come, as in the case of this Conference, an interchange of thought chiefly in aims, methods and results of missionary endeavour, learning from the past and looking to the future. Find where we can work together and then proceed in faith.

The Unfinished Evangelistic Task
Address by Consultant, the Rev. Hans-Ruedi Weber
(World Council of Churches)

A superficial survey of the Church situation in the Southern Pacific could bring us to the conclusion that in this area the evangelistic task of the Church has already been fulfilled or is now rapidly coming to its conclusion. But if one looks below the surface and considers the Church in its total world context, a quite different conclusion will be reached.

I

The Condition of the Church in the World of To-day

In the eyes of God our understanding of Church history, ecclesiastical geography, Church statistics and strategy may be quite wrong. But even a very limited human evaluation of the present condition of the Church in the world is revealing.

1. *The progress of the Gospel through the centuries and continents.* For many centuries Europe was the homeland of the Church. In the Middle Ages European society must have looked very much like Samoan society to-day. It was difficult to draw the distinction between Church and society, because the whole rhythm and structure of everyday life depended upon the rhythm and structure of Church

life. But in the course of the last century, especially since industrialization, the so-called "Christian West" has become a myth rather than a reality. Although an impressive Church facade may still be kept up, the reality is that only a very small percentage of Europeans are active Church members. In Eastern Europe where the Church faces the attack of an athiestic ideology, these Church facades break down and Christians find themselves as a frustrated small minority.

When the European *"corpus Christianum"* first began to break apart, the Christian West made an attempt to conquer the non-Christian world. This series of crusades ended in failure. Only the last of the crusades, the Hispanic conquest in the 15th and 16th centuries, resulted in the Christianization of the whole Latin American continent, which has since become *the* Catholic continent. But to-day it becomes apparent how thin the Christian surface of that continent always was. Despite movements of renewal in Roman Catholicism and the rapidly growing evangelical denominations (especially the Pentecostal movement), the Church is left behind by the far quicker advance of secularism and spiritism.

On the North American continent things seem to look far better. In the pioneer period of American history and on the frontier of the new America in its move towards the west coast, the Church played indeed a vital role. And recently that continent has become famous for its boom in religion. Protestant, Catholic and Jewish places of worship are full. Yet many careful observers warn us that this surge of piety may be moving towards an American culture-religion rather than towards the strengthening of Christ's Church. "The first step towards helping the new America is to realize that the situation has changed, that vital Protestantism in its view of man will be preaching against the vogue, moving against the stream in an environment it had long found congenial." (Martin E. Martin.)

In early Church history (2nd to 7th century) the Church of North Africa played a leading role, before it was wiped out by the hurricane of the Moslem conquest. But since the 18th century in Africa south of the Sahara, a whole army of European and North American missionaries and even more African evangelists have worked and died as witnesses for Christ. Will the fruit of their commitment and suffering be a Christian Africa? Some 10 years ago Bishop Stephen Neill, who has travelled widely in Africa, said: "Around 2000, Africa south of the Sahara may take over the role which has been played earlier in history by 'Christian' Europe". To-day nobody would judge so optimistically. Many observers wonder what will remain of the Church in the midst of the violent outbursts of African nationalism. In the final volume of Growe's monumental history of missions in Africa, the author does not end with the vision of a growing African Christendom, but he deals with "Christian survival" in modern Africa.

The situation of the Church in Asia, that largest and most densely populated continent of our earth, is even more critical. In the first

Christian centuries the Gospel came to Asia (Syrian Church in India),
and it entered China no less than three times (Nestorian Church in
the 6th and 7th centuries, Roman Catholic missions in 13th century
and Protestant and Catholic missions since the 18th century). But
even the tremendous missionary effort of Western churches in modern
times has never resulted in more than tiny minority churches, which
for the most part consist of converts from the more primitive religions.
During the "Vasco da Gama period" these were privileged minorities.
To-day they are only tolerated or even persecuted minorities. And
the Indian historian, K. M. Panikkar, concluded his consideration of
the history of Christian missions in Asia with a chapter on "The
Failure of Christian Missions", in which he states: "It will hardly
be denied that, in spite of the immense and sustained effort made
by the Churches with the support of the lay public of the European
countries and America, the attempt to conquer Asia for Christ has
definitely failed".

This quick survey of the progress of the Gospel through the centuries and continents reveals to us two hard facts about the condition
of the Church in the world of to-day: the Church is to-day a proportionately ever-decreasing minority, and more and more it becomes a
remnant swimming against the current.

2. *A proportionately ever-decreasing minority.* We must face the
fact that almost everywhere in the world of to-day "the Church is
now . . . pursuing its mission at a time when the birth rate is fast
outstripping the conversion rate" (Norman Goodall). In 1900, Christians formed 34% of the total world population. In 1955, they were
only 31%. And if the anticipated birth and conversion rates do not
alter, in the year 2000 Christians will be only 16% of the total world
population.

3. *A remnant swimming against the current.* What is far more
serious is the fact that the tide of world history has turned. A century
ago the Church was seen to be intimately related with the "Christian" Western world; and this Western world had prestige, reached
out into all continents and influenced many cultures. World evangelism seemed to swim with the current of world history.

Since then the "Vasco da Gama period" has come to an end. The
ancient religions are strongly resurging. The scientific revolution has
overthrown many conceptions which are used in the Bible and our
religious language. The Communist conquest has already reached
half the world. And the emerging urban industrial society is radically
different from the former rural society, to which Church life is still
geared. The relatively few Christians left tend therefore to live a
split life: a Christian life on Sundays, in church activities and perhaps in their family where the religious language and criteria may
still be relevant; and a secular life in their daily work where quite
another language is spoken and quite other criteria are followed.
World evangelism to-day must apparently swim against the main
current of world history.

II

A Call to Repentance and Renewal

The above bird's-eye view of the present-day condition of the Church in the world is quite sobering and could make us downhearted and pessimistic. There is a strong temptation to forget about our unfinished evangelistic task and settle down somewhere at the margin of the main stream of life and create there a small Christian world by itself, ignoring our frustrating modern world. But God may very well have brought us into this difficult situation in order to call us to repentance and renewal. He may want to teach us some fundamental lessons about the aim, the agent, and the ways of evangelism. Why do we have to cross the frontier between belief and unbelief? Who is the evangelistic agent? And how are we going to fulfil this evangelistic task?

1. *The aim of evangelism.* When looking at the situation of the Church in the world we have mainly looked at numbers. This is symptomatic. We Christians worship numbers and are bedevilled by the wish to become a majority. When Gideon fought the Midianites, God spoke to him: "The people with you are too many" (Judges 7:2); and God had to repeat once again: "The people are still too many", before Gideon's army was fit for God's war. Perhaps to-day there are too many Christians for the fulfilment of the Church's evangelistic task. God could do more with a mature minority than with an immature majority of Christians. The aim of evangelism is not just the conversion of an ever-increasing number of persons to become members of the Church. Of course we may pray for the conversion of great numbers and join the angels in heaven in their joy when a new soul is drawn out of the kingdom of darkness into the kingdom of light. But we must leave it to God how many or how few He wants to convert, whether and when He wants to increase or decrease the membership of His Church.

I suggest that evangelism is at the same time a humbler and a greater thing than the conversion of more and more people. *We* cannot convert. This is entirely in God's power. Our duty is only to be witnesses. But in this witness we must look beyond the Church towards the ends of the earth and the ends of time. Our witness must bring *all* people and *all* ages and structures of society into a crisis: the whole world (and not only candidates for conversion, few or many) must be faced with the decision for or against Christ. On the other hand, evangelism aims at bringing God's blessing into the total world: the Gospel is the "good news" about God's love for the total world (and not only for the few or many Christians), and signs of this cosmic blessing must be displayed now.

In the fulfilment of this both humble and tremendous evangelistic task, it may be that God elects, calls and converts many or few new members into His Church, but this is not the ultimate aim of evangelism.

Question: Are the above assertions in accordance with the Biblical message? If so: How can we free ourselves from the bedevilling wish to become (or remain) a majority? What does conversion mean according to this conception of evangelism?

2. *The agent of evangelism.* When speaking about the agent of evangelism one usually thinks in the first place of professional missionaries and especially trained evangelists. These certainly have their place in the total mission of God to this world.

I suggest, however, that *the* agent of evangelism is the risen living Lord who is already busy with God's mission in the world. We need not bring Christ into the world, neither into the unevangelised areas remaining, nor into the frustrating new unevangelised sectors of life in industrial society. Christ is already there, judging and redeeming the world. He is already there as the suffering servant and the king incognito. And He calls His Church to join Him in God's mission.

This call is addressed to the total membership of the Church. Every member participates in Christ's mission. Only those who actually live and work in a given environment can both bring this environment into crisis and communicate God's blessing to it. Too much of evangelism happens from outside. As Hendrik Kraemer said, the "communication of" the Gospel is only possible in the context of the "communication between" the evangelist and those to be evangelised. (Note that the evangelist is and remains Christ. If we Christians truly communicate the Gospel to non-Christians, Christ makes the bridge between them and us and teaches both of us.) Every member of the Church shares therefore in this evangelistic task, each at the place where he lives and works according to the gifts of grace which he has received.

Question: Are the above assertions in accordance with the Biblical message? If so: What does the fact that Christ precedes us into the as yet unevangelised areas and unevangelised sectors of life imply for our evangelistic attitude and approach? If the total membership of the Church shares in Christ's mission, what is then the specific task of especially trained and employed missionaries and evangelists?

3. *Ways of evangelism.* When speaking about ways of evangelism we usually turn immediately to special intentional evangelistic activities. We plan for detailed evangelistic campaigns, house-to-house visitation, training and sending out of missionaries and evangelists, new missionary institutions, etc. All this has a place in the fulfilment of our evangelistic task.

I suggest, however, that the total Church life must have an evangelistic dimension. The late Walter Freytag asked many newly-converted Christians during his last Asian journey why they had become Christians. No answer was given to him more frequently than the following: "Christians have another life". Thus these converts made, not in the first place the decision to accept another creed, but the decision to enter into a life, a present reality with which they were confronted while meeting Christians. This other life—according to Freytag—is not in the first place a different moral behaviour, or certainly not only the moral behaviour alone, "but it is another way of life, a life in another *dimension*, a life which stands noticeably under another norm, even if this norm is not obeyed, a life in which another power is at work, which finds expression perhaps only in signs, but always again in a surprising way".

To the fulfilment of the task of evangelism belongs therefore in the first place Christian suffering, Christian worship, Christian community life, Christian service, and then also the spontaneous "gossiping of the Gospel" in the daily conversation of the Church members with their neighbours and workmates. It is primarily this evangelistic dimension which brings the world into crisis and makes the Church a source of blessing.

Only in the context of this spontaneous evangelistic dimension of the total life of the Church will special intentional activities and institutions for evangelism play their proper role.

Question: Are the above assertions in accordance with the Biblical message? If so: How can we strengthen the growth of the evangelistic dimension in the total life of our Church? Which special evangelistic activities and institutions hinder the growth of this evangelistic dimension? And which activities and institutions foster it?

The Relevance of the Gospel to the Changing Conditions of Life in the Pacific
Address by Rev. B. G. Thorogood (Cook Islands)

I

Change is one definition of life—there is no life without some kind of change. The present time of rapid change in the social life of the islands is not a thing to frighten the Church. After all, the Church itself has been the means of some of the most rapid social changes in history. Our task is first to understand the changes that are happening around us. I can only look at the Cook Islands, and may myself be irrelevant to some of you from other areas. There are four aspects of the social change:

1. *Economic change is bringing independence to individuals.* The old basis of economic life was the share which an individual had in the family land. He held this as a life tenant and it gave him the basic means of living—the day-to-day food and a little surplus for trade. It gave a man security, for this was a means of life which could not be easily taken from him. But it was also a form of servitude, almost of slavery, for it bound a man for life to the small circle of existence from which there was no escape. He had to conform to society in order to exist at all.

Now new ways of living are possible. There are many opportunities for regular paid employment—in Government service, in teaching, nursing, in trading, in domestic service; there is a little scope in industry in some places. For all these people the fortnightly pay packet at the Treasurer's Office is more important than the little plot of land. They still have a plot, but probably never work on it themselves—they can get along without it, so long as employment lasts. Although this economic change does not directly affect everyone, it does affect a most important section of the community, and the indirect effects touch the whole community—an alternative way of life is shown to be possible, and to be desirable for many.

The result of this is that for the first time, people are free as individuals to plan their own lives, to build their own homes, to choose their own way of life. They can use their skills, their initiative as never before. They can develop their individual personality. This is a result of economic independence from the family.

2. *The end of the tribe and the beginning of urban life.* The foundation of the chiefly system is power over land and its use. Because the chief was the nominal owner of land in the village, his people had to obey his will and bring him their rent, usually in produce from the land. Under the chief were other ranks, which we, in the Cooks, call *Rangatira* and *Mataiapo,* whose authority was from the chief. We can call this a feudal system, without any hint of condemnation. The great strength of this way of living was that every man had his own place in society with both duties and rights.

He had duties to those above him, to the whole community—in the labour he gave, the ceremonies he observed. He had rights to a share in land and produce, to assistance in sickness and old age. He knew where he stood.

But as soon as people are free to travel from their homes to another island, or to a town, because they no longer depend on their land, then the power of the chief is weakened. The whole tribe loses much of its cohesion. Authority is no longer secure in the same well-known hands. For a long time sentiment remains—"my dear village", etc.—but the authority has gone. In the setting of the town the individual is an anonymous unit without any clear idea of his position in society, no clear duty to others.

In Rarotonga, the centre of Cooks, about half the population is not of Rarotongan birth. People come there for jobs or for educational opportunity or simply because you can rock-and-roll in the dance hall every night. They have effectively cut the strongest link of the tribal unit. In some places we know this as one root of delinquency, that so many people are no longer in the secure position which they occupy in their home village.

3. *Educational advance.* At this time we are seeing the first generation in the Cooks of children with full secondary education, and also a few university graduates. Again this is still a minority, but a powerful one.

In the past the overseas visitor to the islands has been recognized as having authority because of his educational background. Now islanders are stepping into those shoes and have the authority of knowledge and skill, in medicine, in administration, in trade. This is a challenge, not only to the position of the European, but also to the position of the elders in the village. Their authority was built on experience and memory. They said: "We shall plant this tomorrow because the moon is right and the soil is right and we know from the past". Now the educated young expert says: "No, we shall do better to wait, and manure first, then we can get two crops in a year". Such educated people are likely to be very impatient of their elders, regarding as mere magic or mumbo-jumbo the sayings and ceremonies of the elders. Here is a change in the structure of society that can lead to severe strain and tension. Where elders and traditional ways are rigid and dominant and jealous, then the educated young people are likely to show impatience very forcibly. In the Cooks this tension is not likely to be great since the traditional ways of life are already much weakened. But perhaps in Samoa the difficulty may be greater.

4. *The end of isolation.* The Coconut Curtain has been opened, and nothing will ever be quite the same again. This curtain of distance, and ignorance, has for very many years hidden the real condition of the islands from the world; and has hidden the events, the standards, the desires of the world from islanders.

For a long time, we outside the islands have accepted as true the vision of an easy comfortable life without complications. This has hidden from us the real nature of island life. The luxuries which are offered to guests are not a real standard of normal everyday life. In the Cooks there is this facade of great hospitality. Behind it there is still a great deal of poverty, with all the pressures which that means— the bribery which is possible when people are in need ; the burden of debt which accumulates through enforced buying on credit ; the malnutrition of children which belongs to ignorance as much as poverty. These things are there and we ought not to be ashamed of acknowledging them.

But more important, the coconut curtain has parted to show to the islander the nature of Western society. In many places it was the war in the Pacific which did this. Several islands saw the war machine in operation and were caught up in it, with blistering, eye-opening speed. Others, like the Cooks, saw just a military depot, a peaceful occupation force. But it showed very clearly the material values of the Western nations, the kind of people we are *en masse*. Islanders know the things we Europeans long for, and the amount of religion that is lived out among us. With the means of communication which are in use to-day the islands will not be sealed off from the world. For an islander to see all the material benefits which Western nations enjoy, makes him dissatisfied with tradition and is an active agent in change. The minds of people living in the islands are open, and eager for new things.

All this taken together and happening fast amounts to a social revolution.

II

The churches which I know best, and possibly many of the churches we represent, are at present largely irrelevant to this situation.

We are falling behind in the speed of change to-day, so that already for the younger generation, the Church is old-fashioned—after a history of only a hundred years. The Church of Christ lives in the islands by the grace of God, yet the Church itself has become resistant to change so that its life is irrelevant to the changing society. This is perhaps an overstatement, but basically a fair statement of our situation in the Cooks. Why has this happened?

(a) Because historically we have been tied up with the conversion of an island as a whole or a tribe as a whole. The strength of the first evangelism was its appeal to the chief for protection and, when a chief was converted, his people followed him into the Christian world. With that background our Church life has been linked to the life of a village, rather than to the lives of faithful followers of Christ. So when the social pattern changes, the Church is linked to the old and its message is prejudiced and apparently out of touch.

(b) Because we have tended to adopt a hierarchy in the Church parallel to that in the village. (This applies to churches founded by the L.M.S.) We have encouraged people who enter the

Church to see steps of advancement possible before them. We have allowed people to think of the seeker, the member, the deacon, the lay preacher, the ordained pastor, the European missionary as creating a series of steps in rank. This has linked us firmly to the old way of living, where there was this kind of rank.

(c) Because we ourselves have been conservative by nature. Once we have established a tradition we like to think of it as always standing firm. It is as though the Christian community was born in poured concrete—able to change its shape only for a day before it sets firm for ever. Perhaps we are natural conservatives ; certainly we like the solidity of concrete more than the unknown shape of the living cell. So our Christian communities have often shown little of the relevance of the Gospel because they cannot adapt themselves to a new social pattern.

This is all very strange and ironic because the Church itself has been in the past the great force creating social change. A hundred years ago the mission of the Church brought a revolution to the lives of these islands, changing social habits and living conditions more rapidly than the missionaries themselves expected. We rejoice in the power of the Gospel as it has been revealed in the social revolution ; when captives have been released ; when dirt and disease have been fought ; when the lost have been cared for. We rejoice in witness to the Gospel which has been a spearhead of social advance. We are not to-day so proud of the Church when it has sought to defend the *status quo*. We to-day, in danger of being linked to an old social order, need to understand our social patterns and seek God's will in ministering in the midst of such change. It could easily happen that the Church could stand for the past, rather than for the eternal ; we could be so conservative that we cease to be redemptive.

III

Yet if the Gospel is God's truth, and God's action, then it must in fact be relevant to-day. How can we reveal this relevance? I am thinking of some practical ways in which we should direct our efforts. You will probably think of different ways in your society, for the situation is never exactly repeated.

1. *We must stand beside our young people*, those who have entered into the Faith, and who often stand alone. The whole weight of family pressure may be against Christian behaviour and Christian marriage ; we must stand beside the young people even to the extent of helping them disobey their elders. (e.g. Young couple wanting to marry ; forbidden by parents because from wrong village, but agree to cohabitation.) In the past we have stood beside the chiefs with our counsel and care and help. To-day we must do the same for those who are emancipated from the old order and who seek to serve Christ in the new. It is no longer a simple progress from child-

hood in the Sunday School to maturity in Church membership. We cannot assume that this will happen just because the Church exists. We must regard as a top priority the loving care of the young people in the village, so that they will know Christ themselves. They will see the relevance of the Gospel only through a ministry which cares for them and understands their searching minds. Many of our best young people are living in a state of confusion and tension, with the pull of the ancient traditions, the pull of Western materialism and the pull of Christian belief all struggling for the mastery of their hearts. Are we helping them just by saying: "The doors of the church are open and you are invited to worship at 9.00"? They will only find the friend they have in Jesus through the friendship of His servants.

2. *We should reveal the relevance of the Gospel through the fellowship of the Church.* It has been very hard for us to see the true fellowship of the spirit in our churches because the Church is historically a community, a village gathering, with the village elders and the church elders often being the same people, occupying the chief seats at every feast. Yet we know this is not the kind of gathering which deserves the name "fellowship". We should be seeking every means of revealing the Gospel to-day in Christian fellowship, for this is a society where everyone counts, where everyone cares and where everyone is under God's judgement. This is not a chiefly society over again, it is a community of those who love and serve the Lord. Perhaps we must start to reveal this by the way we train those who seek to become members. We have been very weak about this in the past, so that membership has been without any deep understanding of what it means. We have not sought to bring men into a fellowship so much as to enter their names on a membership roll. We have not declared plainly enough the duty of loving service—few of our churches ever dream of having a fund of money to help those in the village who are in need. Yet a few shillings or a few pounds of flour may make all the difference to an old couple hard-pressed through ill health.

3. *We should reveal the relevance of the Gospel through the form of public worship.* Because we come from different traditions we have followed different paths in the ordering of worship. But in any tradition it is easy for worship to become a rite, requiring little thought and little response. It is easy for us to concentrate on getting through the programme rather than hearing the word of the Lord. Yet the worship of the Church should always be relevant to the worshippers. There must somewhere in our worship be the opportunity to bring to God the hard pressing difficulties of our daily lives; to bring thanksgiving for the actual gifts which we are enjoying to-day. Our local worship in the village church should be a means of entering into the Christian inheritance, so that every worshipper sees something of the breadth of Christian experience. Our worship then becomes a living thing when it brings together our

personal experience and the experience of the world Church, and relates both to the living word.

4. *We should reveal the relevance of the Gospel by accepting with thanksgiving the gifts of our island cultures, under the judgment of God.* We do not bring a European Gospel. We give thanks to God for the beauty of the inheritance of each island people. But we state clearly that every culture comes under the searchlight of the Gospel. It is impossible for any outsider to give judgment in this matter and to declare if this particular song or dance or custom is right or wrong. But we should help the Christian community in our islands to make these judgments (which they tend to push on to our shoulders) for themselves, e.g. the Taunga in Cooks—part of the ancient tradition —must be judged by Christians in the islands to see if it is acceptable to the will of God.

5. *We should reveal the relevance of the Gospel by understanding what we mean by salvation and eternal life.* We believe that the work of Christ has to do with all men in their situation as men—as children of God—not with any particular group or type of man ; not with men who are peculiarly aware of sin or who have a strong mystical sense of God. So our preaching of the Gospel must aim at making clear just what is the human situation in which every man lives. If that can carry conviction because of its reality, then the work of Christ for us can be seen not as an old story but as the one thing relevant to our need to-day. I must first know where I stand before I understand what is my way of life. The Gospel always seems irrelevant to those who do not even ask the question: "What am I and what is life all about?" So, to reveal the Gospel as relevant to life means first to declare the nature of human life.

6. *We should reveal the relevance of the Gospel by following the example of our Lord.* His ministry was continually a dealing with actual situations, with real people and their troubles. He did not offer general principles of morality, but spoke to this man's need and that man's sin. To every man he touched He was saving love. He was relevant because His mission and His serving were personal. We have to follow Him and avoid the temptation of dealing with people as a group, with one panacea for all. We follow Him most closely when we are seeking to serve our brother, our neighbour. Only with the spirit of Christ is this kind of relevance possible. He opens our eyes to see what we should be doing for our brother ; He gives us strength to meet the needs of others in the power of His love.

———

There is nothing at all strange in our situation in island life to-day. It is changing rapidly, but that is just the common situation of human life. It is the world we know. We shall be faithful to the Gospel if we carry the marks of the divine life into every aspect of our changing society.

The Relevance of the Gospel to the Changing Conditions of Life in the Pacific

Address by Consultant, the Rev. R. K. Orchard
(International Missionary Council)

Introduction

It is not for me to try to speak about the relevance of the Gospel in actual situations in this Pacific area, since I do not live and work in the area. But the kind of changes we are conscious of in the Pacific area are happening in various degrees and circumstances everywhere in the world. Everywhere the ways in which we have been accustomed to do things are changing, because of the effects of industry, of new technical knowledge and methods, of the rapid communication of ideas, of the mixing up together of people of different ways of life. The goals of life together in any particular community, once taken for granted, are now being questioned and altered.

I think the first time I realized this vividly was on the first visit I made to Central Africa, now some fifteen years ago. Walking across a mission station, I met an old man going hunting armed with a bow and arrow. I had my first and last lesson in archery. He and his bow and arrow are gone now. Twenty-four hours later I found myself being driven along a tarmacadam road with electric lights and pit-head gear dominating the sky, past the longest conveyor belt in the southern hemisphere. From bow and arrow to conveyor belt is twenty-four hours' journey. Africa has moved in a generation from communal land ownership to the individualism of the pay packet; from wondering how to avoid the hunger period in the year to strikes for higher wages.

Amidst changes like that—though not always so dramatic—the churches all over the world are seeking to understand what it means to express the Christian Gospel through their life and witness in such changing circumstances. They are trying to understand afresh *what* the Gospel says to men in the midst of the new ways of living together, and what it has to say about those new ways. They are also asking themselves how they can make the Gospel plain in ways which will be meaningful in the midst of these new ways.

Since this is going on all over the world, a consultant can perhaps help the thinking and discussion of this Conference about this subject within the Pacific area by sharing some thoughts gained from some acquaintance with the discussion of it in some other parts of the world, because it is *one* Gospel which we seek to live by, understand and express.

I

Reasons why the Gospel is relevant to changing conditions

Let us first of all remind ourselves that the Word which God has spoken to us in Jesus Christ is not a word for one set of circumstances only, which loses its meaning if those circumstances change. It is God's word for all men, everywhere, in all circumstances. Why is this so?

(1) First, I believe, because this is God's world. This is a hard thing to believe in a world of nuclear bombs and space ships. But the great fact of our age is not that a man has been launched into space; it is that this is A.D., the Year of the Lord—that we live in an age into which Christ has come and of which he is the hidden king. Christians have always found the whole meaning of life summed up and expressed in Jesus Christ. In Him they have found what life is all about. And when they have tried to express that meaning, they have found that it stretches out and out from that centre, until it takes in all human history and the physical universe which is history's stage. We believe this is God's world because it is in this created world that Jesus Christ lived and died and rose again. God does not speak with contradictory voices, one in the world He created and another in Jesus Christ. He speaks one word. We have heard it in Jesus Christ and so we can hear it in the world God created and over which He rules. This is the testimony of John's Gospel: "In the beginning was the Word, and the Word was with God and the Word was God. . . . and the Word became flesh and dwelt among us": and of the letter to the Christians in Colossae: "For in Christ were all things created in the heavens and upon the earth, whether thrones or dominions or principalities or powers: all things have been created through him and unto him and he is before all things and in him all things consist". (Col. 1:16.)

It was into this world—which also contains nuclear bombs and space ships—that God came in Jesus Christ; not into some other world. The Gospel is good news of God's entry into *this* life which we live as human beings, into this history of which we—and pit-head gear and conveyor belts—are part. The Gospel isn't *only* about what goes on inside ourselves, or about us as individuals or about another life than this one, though it does speak about all these things. It is first of all about the world, and about what God had done in it, supremely in Jesus Christ who lived and died and rose again in it, and about its goal, that all things are to be summed up in Him.

Because this event of Jesus Christ is the centre of history, and happened in the midst of human existence, it speaks to us as men, as human beings whether we live in the Pacific or in Africa or in Europe; whether we live in the space age or the iron age or the stone age, Jesus Christ is the great contemporary of every age.

I remember a journey in Africa some years ago which began in the South and showed me the skyscraper and mine dumps of Joburg, where seventy years ago was just rolling grassland, and took me across the dry and arid spaces of Bechuanaland—most of which is the Kalahari desert in the remote parts of which the little bushmen wander, and brought me on past the cooling towers of Bulawayo's electrical generating station to the Copper Belt of Northern Rhodesia which thirty years ago was primeval bush; and on from there to the then still remote N.E. Rhodesia and its village life and subsistence agriculture and fishing.   There, in the freshness of early morning, I went to the mud-walled thatched village church and watched little groups of Africans coming up the hill to share in Christian worship. An African minister was taking the service and it was in Mambure, a language I could not understand.   But towards the end he took bread and broke it and handed it round; and took a cup and drank and passed it on.   I could understand that—the acts that express the Gospel in action and which speak to Christians whatever their language.   And behind that bread it seemed to me I could see the mealie lands of the Transvaal and the cassava gardens of Northern Rhodesia; yes, and the gold of the Rand and the copper of the Copper Belt—and behind the cup, the water which means life in Africa from the boreholes and dams of the dry Kalahari and the rivers and lakes of N. Rhodesia.   My mind went northwards up the great lake Tanganyika—up that great Rift Valley of the Nile and the Dead Sea and Galilee.   Here were Christians getting their life not from the West but from that event in Palestine which was also an event happening amongst them, and beginning to bring mealies and cassava, gold and copper, the stuff of the common life, under obedience to the Living Christ—beginning to recognize in Him the living centre, the transforming centre of *all* life.

II

The calling of Christians to make plain the relevance of the Gospel

But that congregation in rural N. Rhodesia consisted mostly of women and children and a few old men.   When one asked where were the younger men, the answer was they had gone off to work at the mines—thereby incidentally disrupting the pattern of village life. What does it mean to celebrate the Lord's Supper amidst such changes?   How is the meaning of the Gospel made relevant to them?

(a) In one sense the answer is that it isn't!   Christians are not called to make the Gospel relevant.   To attempt to do that is to make the Gospel merely adjectival to something else, tacked on to it as an appendage.   To attempt to do so is to try to make use of God.   There are people who try to use the Christian religion in this way—to use it as a way of sticking together the bits of a social order that is falling apart, or to use it to bring about changes in a social order which they desire for other reasons.   Christians have tried to do that kind of thing at many points in history and they are tempted to do it to-day.   There are some people in Britain who say: "Our social order is disintegrating.   Look at the breakdown of respect for property rights; look at the breakdown of family life; look at the delinquency amongst young people.   Let's try a spot of religion and see if that will stop the rot"—which is to say, let's make use of God. I once heard a group of African Christians in a part of Africa where they were striving for political independence, singing fervently

Luther's hymn *"A safe stronghold our God is still"* and I could not help wondering who they had in mind when they used the second person plural—*"our* God—He'll help *us* free from all the ills which have *us* now o'ertaken". Were they thinking of all the people of God everywhere? Or did the "us" mean "us Africans"? Were they trying to use God for their own ends?

In fact, the Christian Gospel is not adjectival to anything. It is unashamedly indicative, making statements about what God has done —"God so loved the world that He sent His Son"; "God was in Christ reconciling the world to Himself". Because the Gospel is news about the central act at the heart of all history, it does not have to be *made* relevant: it *is* relevant.

(b) So the calling of Christians is to live by and through the Gospel in the midst of men's living together. That sounds obvious: but it is astonishing how easily we use Christianity as a way of escape from really living in the life of this world. We make it into something concerned only with our inner life; or an activity which goes on in church which has no connection with what goes on in the field or the factory or the workshop; or something whose only purpose is to rescue us from this life in the workaday world into some other life —almost as though it said to us: "If you keep the rules, you will be safely tucked up somewhere out of harm's way". Perhaps this is part of what was in Peter's mind when Jesus told him that He was going to be crucified and Peter said: "Be it far from thee, Lord. This shall never be to thee" and Jesus told him that this was the spirit of Satan in him and that he was taking care for the things of men, not the things of God.

Yet it was into this human existence of prostitutes and get-rich-quick types, of political expediencies and executions that Jesus came. If we are to be His people it is in the workaday life of the world and all its ordinary relationships that we must be His people. But we can only be His people if we recognize that He came *into* this world—into it from outside it. We are not allowed as Christians to be wholly absorbed in this present era, or to find the centre of our loyalty in it. We are bidden to seek first God's kingdom, not any human kingdom. We are strangers and pilgrims on the earth.

This means that we have to be wisely and constructively critical both of any social order in which we find ourselves, and of changes which are taking place in it, and we do so from a standing ground which is detached from both. For instance, when I speak about these things in Britain, I suggest that we as Christians in Britain have to be critical of and resistant to most of the advertising that goes on on radio and T.V. and newspapers, because it is constantly setting before men a picture of what makes the good life which the understanding of the good life which the Gospel gives us compels us to criticize. The good life as pictured by modern mass advertising reflects standards in our contemporary social order and also seeks to change them, and neither the standards nor the changes are such that Chris-

tians can accept them. Mass advertising suggests that a man's life
does consist in the abundance of things which he has; it tries to
persuade him that he needs more and more. It suggests that we have
a right to comfort and luxury and ease. It suggests that a man's
worth is measured by the size of his house and his car—symbols of
status and prestige. That's a picture of the good life which Christians
can't accept. It is one that perhaps is not confined to Britain. Nor
are its Christian critics. I remember an African minister in whose
ordination I was privileged to share. Like most ministers in that
part of Africa, he had been a teacher. If he had stayed on teaching
he would have got a much bigger salary than the very small one he
received as a minister. In his ordination statement, he said: "I am
often asked why I have given up the prospect of a much better salary
for the comparative poverty of a minister. I know I shall never be
rich as a minister. But I have discovered that there are no riches
like those in Jesus".

So we as Christians are called to the difficult task of being at once
involved in the life of the community round about us and detached
from it. Involved, because Jesus Christ is involved; it was in the
midst of an actual human community, in its relationships and pressures that He lived and died and rose again. Detached, because He
was detached, with the loneliness of one who came from another
kingdom than the kingdoms of this age, and whose followers even
at their last meal with Him did not understand what He was about,
and who in the end had that final detachment of Resurrection which
bursts all our human categories with a new life, a new creation, the
life of the age to come present in the here-and-now, and who calls
us to share that new life by sharing what a South African Senator
recently described as "the tremendous minority of the Cross".
(E. H. Brookes.)

III

The requirements of the calling

It is hard to be loyal to this double-sided calling. There are, I
believe, two essentials if we are to be kept loyal to it.

The first is to be rooted in the Gospel—to return time and time
again to that Event which is the incarnation, teaching and ministry,
death and resurrection of Jesus Christ and all that is linked with it
in the preparation of the children of Israel and all that flows from
it in the gathering of Christ's people into His Church.

This is required both of individual Christians and of churches. It
is required of churches if churches are to have this relationship of
responsible detachment to the communities in which they are set, if
they are to be involved without being identified with the community,
if they are to be distinct from it without being irresponsible towards
it. This means that the structure of a church's life must be a testimony to the Gospel; the way it orders its worship, the way it orders

its life through church meetings and assemblies, diocesan councils, the district and conference—whatever they are called in different traditions—must be such as to be a testimony to the Gospel and to help to keep the life of the Church centred in the Event of Jesus Christ. This means also that the way a church lives its life within that structure—the place it gives to the Bible in its worship and its decisions, the way in which it nurtures its members, the kind of thing it regards as important and to which it gives time and energy and money— these things must be such as reflect the Event and build up the life of the Church in obedience to it.

These things—the structure of a church's life and the way it lives its life within that structure—are not matters to be decided by what the members or the leaders of a church like, or are accustomed to, or by what happens to suit the ways of a particular community or the outlook of a particular period. They are to be decided by bringing our church life, in its structure and in its practice, constantly under the correction of the Gospel. Insofar as we seek to keep our life together within a church open and obedient to the Gospel, God will through His Holy Spirit make our church into a real school of living together, a working model, so to say, of the community. The influence of churches which are true communities in Christ will spread outwards as a creative influence in the wider community in which they are set. Is not this part of what Jesus meant when He told His followers they were to be like salt, like light, like a city which is set on a hill?

This is a consequence which flows from church life lived under the Gospel. I have seen some signs of it here and there in Africa, where Africans have carried into public life insights and habits learned in the community of the church—e.g. how to use responsibly church funds, and so have carried responsibility and integrity into public life ; and how to conduct business in church assemblies in ways which both lead the Christian community to sound decisions and yet do not suppress minorities who hold different views conscientiously, and so have brought to political life maturity and capacity for genuine leadership. I think the same process can be seen at work in the story of the churches in many countries. For instance, the development of political institutions in Britain owes much to, for example, the practice of the church meeting in the early days of Congregationalism and to the Methodist class meeting and lay preaching tradition. But note again that these things are by-products, not the aim of the ordering of church life. To aim to order church life *in order* that it may be a school of community living is to ruin it. The calling of churches is to bring their lives constantly under obedience to the Gospel for the sake of the Gospel, and not for any secondary reason.

How a church keeps its life obedient to the Gospel is a big subject. Churches of different traditions would give different answers to that question—answers which would differ in emphasis and in a few points in substance. But I think we should all agree that one essential is to use faithfully the means which God has provided for the upbuilding of the life of His Church—Worship, the Scriptures, the mutual responsibility of members for one another in their life in the Church.

I remember once attending Sunday worship with an African congregation which met in a mine compound in Johannesburg. A sympathetic compound manager had put a room at their disposal where they used to gather on a Sunday morning and be visited whenever possible by a lay pastor who led their simple worship of praise and prayer and Bible reading and preaching. It was the custom of the mine also to provide on Sunday an opportunity for traditional African tribal dancing—a form of recreation of which Africans are very fond —so that different tribal groups dressed in traditional costumes would dance in a big open space watched by a large crowd, who were soon joining in. Consequently, the worship of this congregation was penetrated by the drumming and shouting of the dance. There was a third group amongst the mine employees which did not join either in the dancing or the worship. It despised both—religion it thought achieved nothing and tribal dances belonged to the past. This group thought it was emancipated from both. But as I shared in the worship of that little Christian congregation, I thought to myself: "This is at the centre of things. This group is finding renewal, re-creation, neither by trying to escape momentarily from to-day's world into yesterday's, nor by trying to escape into a world of to-morrow under the illusion that men are thought to be self-sufficient. But, in the midst of to-day, it is opening itself to the living centre from which a new community can grow and in the light of which men can learn what it means to be not submerged in a mass nor lost in an illusory self-sufficient individualism but truly human."

But churches are not only the people of God gathered into the structure of ordered church life. Churches are also the people of God dispersed in daily life, scattered so to say amongst all the daily occupations of men and amongst all their relationships in human society. They are bus drivers and storekeepers, teachers and agricultural workers, nurses and factory workers: they are also members of families, and citizens of countries. It is through Christians scattered in the life of the world that the relevance of the Gospel to daily life in its changing forms can be most clearly and concretely manifested. It is part of our calling as Christians to live our lives in our daily occupations and relationships as those who know that this is God's world of which Jesus Christ is both the centre and the goal. This is easy to say and hard to do. These spheres of human living—industry and commerce, the professions, political life—are organized round other centres and are striving for other goals. These other centres and goals are not necessarily incompatible with the Lordship of Christ. They are at best partial and incomplete and if they are regarded as ends in themselves they deny the sole Lordship of Jesus Christ and become spheres of idolatry. So there is always tension between a Christian's commitment to Christ and the claims which his job and his relationship make upon him.

Let me give but one example. Many of my friends in Africa are involved in one way or another in politics—some because it is their full-time work as leaders in political parties or as government servants, some because they are members of political parties. In all that realm of life which we gather under the term politics they are involved with matters of power, because politics is concerned with the exercise of power—power in the direct sense of coercive power. That naturally sets up a tension with their Christian commitment to Christ, whose power was not the power of coercion but the different power of self-giving and suffering. There are some amongst the leaders of the churches in Africa who draw the deduction that Christians should keep out of politics. "It's a dirty game," they say. "You'll only be corrupted if you get involved." "But," say my African friends—and I think rightly, "if some Christians don't serve in political life from a sense of Christian vocation, then the whole realm of politics will just be handed over to those who have no Christian commitment, who will make the exercise of coercive power an end in itself and politics, which in its widest sense affects so much of life to-day, will become a realm increasingly resistant to the Lordship of Jesus Christ. But," my friends go on to say, "we do need the help of our fellow Christians in living the Christian life in this sphere. We need their help in understanding what it means to be loyal to Jesus Christ in political life and in making the very difficult decisions we have to make out of a Christian obedience". Many of these people are desperately lonely and have a real hunger for Christian companionship in their calling. And it's not only Christians in political life who feel this need—it's also the most thoughtful Christians in education, in medicine, in industry and commerce. Isn't it part of the job of churches to seek to meet this need, to provide e.g. occasions when Christians in industry can meet together to talk about their Christian life in industry, freely and frankly, and see what can be learned together from the Gospel about the meaning of work and about labour relations and about personal relations with fellow workers, and so on with the other spheres in which Christians are involved? Is it not part of the task of the churches to provide training for their members not simply in what it means to be a Christian in private life, so to say, but also in the life out in the world, in daily work, as a citizen, as a participant in the economic life of the community, and so on?

We mustn't fall into the error of supposing that Christ provides a set of ready-made answers. We can't produce a neat little set of textbooks for this and that department of life from which church members can look up ready-made answers for all their questions. The Gospel provides an ultimate commitment and a perspective for daily living, not a set of rules. We live by faith not by rules and in the end we must take responsibility for our decisions. Nor should

we suppose that a Christian commitment is an excuse for not knowing and realizing the technical facts of any particular sphere of
activity. If I take a ride on a bus I expect the driver to know how
the gears and steering work, and if he runs into a tree, I won't
accept it as a valid excuse if he says that he's a practising Christian!
Christians won't commend the Gospel unless they are good at their
jobs. But there is help which the churches can provide in the concrete problems of daily living by giving training in the understanding
of the Christian life in the context of daily work in the contemporary
world and particularly in the provision of opportunities for Christians
to discuss their daily life together and help one another with their
decisions, provided the churches understand that Christians live their
lives as Christians dispersed in the world as well as gathered in church
and are prepared to be alongside their members in their life in the
world. It is in some such ways as these that churches can help to
build up that inner disciplined life of Christians which gives stability
and consistency in their response to Jesus Christ in their living in
the world.

Conclusion

In this calling of Christians to manifest the relevance of the Gospel
amidst changes going on around us, there is, as we have seen, always
a tension for us. If we don't feel that tension, then I suggest there
is something lacking in our church life. We cannot escape that
tension and we ought not to try to do so. For we are called to live
in two worlds, or two eras (*aeon* is the New Testament word) at
once. We live in this present historical age of our human existence
along with our fellow men, and we are bound up with them. We
have no right to try to contract out of it, for that would be to
repudiate the incarnation. At the same time, we live in the age of
the new creation which Jesus Christ inaugurated and we share in the
new manhood which is his gift. It is in this new age that our ultimate loyalty, our final commitment and our real life rest. It is our
calling to manifest that new life within this present age. This is
difficult and costly. It is possible only because Christ died and rose
again, and through the Holy Spirit we can share that dying and rising
life here and now. It is this faith which enables us to carry this
tension, not escaping it by simply trying to live wholly within one
age or the other, but bearing the Cross which stands at the meeting
place of both. Paul sums it up in the letter we are studying in
words which are for me one of the most profound and moving
descriptions of the Christian life ever written:
> "I have been crucified with Christ: yet I live: and yet no
> longer I, but Christ liveth in me and that life which I now
> live in the flesh I live in faith, the faith which is in the Son
> of God, who loved me and gave himself up for me."
>   Gal. 2:20.

The Place of Young People in the Life of the Church
Outline of Address by Rev. Ta Upu Pere (*Cook Islands*)

I

The Past. What do we recollect when we glance back and make a brief survey about the life of the Church some forty to sixty years ago?

(a) The young people of those days are mothers and fathers of to-day. We of the young people of to-day learn from our parents of incidents in the past life of the Church—its growth, its progress, its drawbacks, etc.

(b) The fellowship of the Church was then regarded as a place for all ages within the community; but the tragic thing was that the young people had no opportunity to express their own feelings and ideas. It was taken for granted that the youngsters had to wait until they became deacons or pastors before they could say anything in the meetings.

(c) The Sunday School was the only place where any child or youngster could speak in public.

(d) Many remained all their lives in the Sunday School. They learned and sat together with their grandchildren in Sunday School lessons.

II

The Present. What do we see in the life of the Church to-day?

(a) The fathers and mothers of the young people of to-day are slow in changing their attitude about young people and their place within the life of the Church. Slow also to accept the changing conditions of the material world.

(b) The old people are afraid to lose their dignity, their prestige; they cling to Church traditions governed by ancient laws and rules— some good and some very crude. There seems to be envy and jealousy in the hearts of the adult leaders of the Church to-day whenever a young man or woman stands up to speak in a meeting in the Church.

III

The Future. Are we prepared to take the initiative in training our own young people and children and allowing them to see for themselves their place not as members only but as future leaders within the life of the Church?

(a) Our young people are moving speedily ahead, following the pattern of this fast-moving modern world of ours. We are afraid to follow them. Then we lose them to the world. We shout after them, and have been shouting too long, far away up in the pulpit. It is about time we came down and showed our young people that we are willing to help them.

(b) There is a feeling in the minds of the young people that the

Church fellowship is only for the old people with their old Book—
the Bible. We have clung too long to our old ways of thinking
and old ideas and methods.

(c) I feel the young people see their place in the life of the Church
but we are afraid to admit it. Jesus said: "I must be about my
Father's business".

The Place of Young People in the Life of the Church

Outline of Address by Consultant, U Kyaw Than
(*East Asia Christian Conference*)

I

The Topic. My address on this sub-topic has necessarily to be based
on some related statements made by Asian Christian youth at Asian
conferences or meetings, and on some of my own experiences in
personal contacts with Asian youth in general. Yet it is hoped that
in the course of the address some notes will also be struck relevant
to the Christian situation in the Pacific area.

Speaking out of such a background, I'd prefer to have the topic
changed around a bit to underline certain emphases. The question is
not whether youth should be not only *seen* but also *heard* at church
meetings—not merely how youth could be *retained* in the churches.
Rather it is the whole question of integrating youth, not only in the
life, but in the life and mission of the Church in the world.

And we should not think of pastoral care to Christian young people
only, but also of *witnessing* for Christ among *all* young people in
our lands. Hence the topic might be considered not so much in
terms of the place of Christian young people in the life of our
churches, but of *the mission of the Church to all young people in our
lands.*

II

The Situation of Youth To-day

(a) In a few countries of Asia some national leaders are of youthful
age and were called up from the ranks of youth leadership to help
to hold the helm of the state—a number of Christian congregations
in Japan, Indonesia and Burma are substantially made up of young
people.

(b) When churches appear to be thinking of their own affairs as
groups or institutions, young people are not likely to be interested
in the Church. But when the Church grapples with the problems of
her mission to the changing society in which she is placed by God,
then young people tend to sit up and listen and also participate in
her mission. The revolution in contemporary society is a challenge
to the Church to speak the prophetic Word to youth in the perplexi-
ties of modern national life. Young people will look to the prophetic
Church for *Christian discernment in the national upheavals of our*

times. "Young people are caught up between the tension of national aspirations on one hand and loyalty to their faith on the other. For instance, in Japan, many young people go to the Church to become Christian, because that seems to be the highlight of modernization. But many of them soon find it very uncomfortable in the Church, and they leave it never to come back. This was also true of young soldiers after the war, seeking a spiritual backbone which they lost during the war. The reason why those young soldiers went to the Church was to seek for direction and to try to find out their responsibilities in the rapidly changing society. They were trying to adopt only the moral teaching from the Bible, but they did not meet the living Christ."

(c) Further, the mission of the Church to all young people in our lands will have to go hand in hand with *Christian discernment in the cultural crisis of our times.* The cultural crisis arises out of the situation that the world is growing smaller through air travel, radio and television. No corner of the earth can escape for long the impact of outside influences. In Asian lands it is manifested in the encounter between "traditional" culture and that of modern science and technology. The old cultural values are often questioned in face of the new, and all young people—Christian and non-Christian —are searching for landmarks to guide their behaviour in contemporary society.

(d) And there is confusion between *Western culture* and Christianity. Sensitive young people are not satisfied that adoption of Christian faith implies adoption of Western culture.

The discernment in the light of the word of God of the "landmarks" the young people are looking for is an urgent need in the mission of the Church to all young people to-day.

(e) In this connection, the confusion and uncertainties in the encounter between traditional culture and modern technology are further aggravated by the downright *"secularism"* which arises in the process of this encounter. It disposes of religion as irrelevant and sets aside "spiritual concerns" as outmoded inhibitions of unprogressive man. It makes the modern and progressive man feel that he hasn't really got to worry about "religion" and "spiritual concerns" any more.

(f) Added to the above are the effects of the second world war, post-war national revolutions and internal strife within the newly developing nation states. The system of Christian instruction for each rising generation is particularly affected, and unless we watch carefully we may soon discover that our churches are made up of members of the new generations of *religious illiterates,* to whom the Incarnation, the Crucifixion of Christ and His redemption of the world may be mere meaningless articles of faith which had some sentimental value for the old people at one time.

(g) All these are applicable to the situation of both young men and *young women* in our lands. New secularism also affects relations between young men and young women in their new-found social freedom. It is the task of the Church to help young people in the *Biblical* understanding of "marriage", "family" and "home" in the changing societies of our lands.

(h) *The use of leisure*. With the coming of technological advance, young people of our day are finding more leisure on their hands than those of the past. We may add to this the economic situation of some lands where "unemployment" is a problem. Unemployment either due to economic conditions or uncreative leisure due to progress can be the devil's opportunity, unless the Church in an understanding and imaginative way renders pastoral care to these youth. I am not proposing that the Church should arrange for more worship services directed to youth! Rather this should require very serious prayer and thought on the part of the whole Church.

These notes I have presented on the situation of young people to-day are, all except two, based on the statements made by Christian youth at the Inaugural Assembly of the East Asia Christian Conference (EACC) at Kuala Lumpur, Malaya, in 1959, and more recently at Bangkok where the EACC Youth Committee met.

III

The Church's Response

If our young people—inside or outside the churches—are in these situations, then the Church's response to these needs cannot be merely in terms of the concern to "retain" or "conserve" Christian young people within her fold. "Youth have to be a part of the Church, and the Church must go where the youth are found." Her response cannot be a reluctant response, grudgingly given, due to unavoidable demands of the changing times. It cannot be one of more "conservation" and giving *some* place to young people in her life (e.g. in worship) to make them feel they have some part to play. Rather the concern for youth must be seen as belonging to her *act of obedience* to the One who is calling her to mission among all the young people of the land where God has placed her.

The Church is the "household of faith" where both the old and the young are found together. It is not the monopoly of the one or the other. *"The youth have been among the first to meet the challenge of Christianity.* From the days of Jesus to our century, young men and women have answered the call of the Church. The great missionary movement of the 19th century that brought the gospel to our shores has been to a large extent due to the vision of the youth of that day."

"It would not be wrong to say that the youth movements and the student movements working among Christian young people set in motion the ecumenical movement." Youth, provided with *opportunities for contacts* with *Christian young people beyond one's own borders, both national, geographical and denominational*, had been fired by the imagination and vision of the Church universal and their

Christian faith deepened, and vision broadened through such encounters. Leaders have emerged from the ranks of youth helping as stewards or ushers at international Christian conferences and consultations. *Leadership training* through courses is a continuing need in our lands. This would also promote closer contact and mutual sharing of experience among our churches in their common ministry to our youth. *Work-camps* were introduced in Asia about twelve years ago. Between 1949-59, fifty-two camps were held in nine countries in the area, attended by more than 2,000 youth. These have not only served in the reconstruction of church and other institutions, but have also helped remove prejudice, hatred and other evils created by the last world war.

Indigenous Literature. Much of the youth literature found in our lands is either an importation or adaptation. There is a great need for indigenous literature, speaking to the problems and challenges of our own young people.

There is a need for taking seriously the presentation of the gospel to youth and this requires special prayer and thought. Witness to *youth requires proper recognition* in the mission and ministry of the Church and a reflection on its significance in our present Church budgets may throw some light on the special importance we attach or don't attach to it.

Unity. Where youth work exists we feel there is a need for coordinating it among the churches of our nations. This will not only avoid overlapping and duplication, but help the youth groups of various churches to understand each other and get inspiration from one another. The problem in some situations is the presence of divergent youth groups claiming the loyalty of youth. The sectarian influence is very strong and is taking youth away from the Church in many countries.

IV

Conclusion

We can see that speaking of the needs and concerns among youth leads us on to all kinds of urgent issues the whole society and the whole Church are facing these days. What are we doing to integrate youth and the concern for youth into the total mission of the Church? Are we just aiming to keep them out of the world? Are we only counting and trying to "conserve" the few fishes "the Church" has caught, or are we launching out into deeper waters with Christ to cast forth His salvation? The Church is called to understand her true nature and purpose in Christ. The presentation of the gospel to youth and the place of youth in the mission of the Church may be likened to that act of Elisha the prophet in II Kings 2:21 when he "cast the salt at the spring of waters". For Christian witness to youth in our days may be one of the most strategic tasks of the Church in contemporary society. For, tell me the situation of Christian witness among youth to-day, and I will tell you the future of the Church's life and mission in society to-morrow.

The Christian Family

Address by Rev. S. Raapoto (Tahiti)
(translated from the French)

Although I have undertaken the task of introducing the topic "The Christian Family", it is not because I possess any special competence for discussion in this field, although I am the father of a large family! When Mr. Orchard, in his letter at the beginning of the year, asked me to present this subject, my first impulse was to refuse. This was not because the theme of "The Family" is not one for serious study but because I felt myself unequal to such a task, because I already had heavy duties in the Tahitian Church and also, and I say this with some sorrow, because family and marital ties as envisaged from a Christian standpoint are to-day suffering a serious testing time in our islands, particularly since the introduction from the Western world of an excessive moral freedom which thwarts and silently undermines the slow growth of Christian behaviour amongst our people.

Now please do not think that we wish to hide anything, nor that we are not anxious to participate to the full extent of our limited ability in this Conference! You will perhaps excuse the somewhat special way in which this report is presented and also any omissions.

I

Let us see how the family and marriage appear in the actual situation of our islands of the W. Pacific. I shall have to refer, during this study, to the state of affairs which I find in French Polynesia, rather than to conditions in other parts of the Pacific which I have not as yet the pleasure of knowing. The information about each other which we have all read in the preparatory documents for this Conference has been of great value for comparison and each of us can find there both similarities and differences, all of which, however, I think, arise from a common basis of social and ethnic climate.

The indigenous population of French Polynesia has been Christian for many years. After the very difficult pioneer work of the missionaries of the London Missionary Society, there came a very great change—official acceptance of the Gospel, unification of the country, codification of the language through the translation of the Bible into Tahitian, the abandonment of pagan morals and customs, and a desire to learn to read in order to read the Bible. This revolution was effected not by individuals but by co-operation. All was done in the context of an *"esprit de groupe"* and hardly ever through the reflection of an individual personality. Evangelists and pastors nearly always laid down precise methods of working and ruled their people more like chiefs than winners of souls. The Bible was considered a Sacred Book, rather than the living Word of God. It would probably have been impossible for those in charge of the first Christian communities to have acted otherwise, when men were reaching out from the stone age, from the bosom of the tribe, and emerging into a nineteenth century very pleased with itself! What they were able to understand, they took over—often with very happy results—into the framework of the new customs, renewed in the light of the Gospel.

One must not be too surprised if questions as difficult as Christian family and marriage, upbringing and culture, *"de la maniere des blancs"*, gave rise to imitation rather than real, properly understood assimilation. Even to-day, the Tahitian, although he quickly adapts himself to those aspects of modern life which please him, for example those which make living easier, finds it much more difficult to enter the world of longstanding civilization. Very attracted by novelties, he nevertheless quickly returns to his own ways. The old method of imposing acceptance had its value ; to-day it has lost its effectiveness. We are involved in a very sharp contrast—return towards a past which can never return, attraction towards modern superficial living. And here is the tragedy—that the power of the Gospel to salvation has not penetrated sufficiently deeply into hearts and consciences for there to arise from amongst the people heralds of the Truth, prophets and saints!

The basic element in family life in our islands of Polynesia, even stronger than blood ties, is that of *subsistence*. The family gathering is where one finds one's food, where it is prepared and where all can satisfy their hunger, whether they belong closely or loosely to the group. All who feel more or less attached to the group feel at home there. For instance, one may go to a distant island without warning and know that one will be taken in. Sometimes as many as thirty persons live together and to-day in Papeete it is not uncommon to see several different families living in the same place with a communal life centred round the provision of food.

The custom of *adoption* (*faamu*—to give to eat) arises from this basic foundation and sometimes surpasses blood ties. A child adopted at birth is bound to those adopting it as strongly as one of their own children. This custom still exists in many parts of the Pacific. At first the idea was that families with children should give some of them to families with none. But later this custom was extended and enlarged and became a sort of infant-exchange. One bespeaks well in advance a child that is to be born into a certain family, and at birth one takes it away. The child will enjoy the same rights as the true children of one's family and will be even more petted than the others. The aim used to be to secure the union of two families or family groups and perhaps by this means increase their influence. To-day this custom is very widespread, even amongst families connected with the Church. This is a delicate problem for a really Christian conception of the family, and only by careful action can the Church effect some change in this field. It is noticed that none of the Pacific communities have mentioned the problem of adoption in the Christian Family, and we shall be glad to know how this custom, if it exists, has been resolved by others.

A second element which one finds at the base of family groups is that of the *extended family,* in rather the same way as there used to be the *"gens romana".* The family comprises not only the father, mother, children—true or adopted, the father's parents, the mother's parents, but men and women who live with the family and who are cared for in return for help in the various duties of the house. To this first group is then added a group of those closely or distantly related —uncles, aunts, cousins by birth or by marriage, all those with whom one has any family ties are united in the family group; this is the *"fetii".* A child scarcely distinguishes his father from the other men of the family, whom he will call "Papa". The uncle and the father will be called by the same name: *"Metua".* (It is important to notice that the uncle preserves a special right concerning his nephews and feels very closely linked with them.) Brothers and sisters are on a par with cousins, and the same word is used for both: *"taeae".*

This *"gens polynesiensis"* is not closed and fixed; it changes constantly and each day sees something new. A family grows and then splits up. It takes in new members and loses others. Some leave, occasionally without intending to return; others arrive and instal themselves. All this seems normal and the children are not surprised by changes. All those who sleep under the same roof become part of the family at the precise moment that they come together. During the day they disperse and at night re-form into a different family; new arrivals replace those who have left. This is particularly useful in towns and places of permanent or temporary meeting—ports, pearl-diving islands, times of festivity, etc. Movement is less free in the villages of the isolated archipelagos where a certain fixed society remains. But there, as elsewhere, the spirit of the group is stronger than the spirit of the family.

A further idea needs to be introduced to understand the Polynesian family: this is the idea of *equality.* We have said that from birth the child is cared for by its mother, and often the father will take over these duties. As it grows older, the child becomes a toy, loved but not trained. When the child can eat alone, nobody bothers with it any more; its brothers and sisters watch over it. It grows up in the house without anybody really caring for it. Nobody displays any feeling for it. This equality in the house, this lack of degree, this absence of feeling and even of respect towards the child, means that the child has a life almost on the fringe of the family and will himself have a lack of respect for his parents—all the more when in the communal bedroom the elders do not mince matters in conversation. Initiated very early into the mysteries of life, without however understanding them, he sees quarrels, hears jokes and adult conversations, and is sometimes even invited to imitate his parents in indecent dances. It is, of course, important not to generalise too hastily; we shall see what a Tahitian family can be when it knows its duty. But the situation is very often like this in our Polynesian isles.

Up to now, we have discussed general ideas underlying the reality of the family. Although the clan or Tribe has not existed for some time, there is still this group spirit from which springs the sociability and peculiar charm of the Polynesian character. In former days there was the chief of the clan or tribe; to-day there are the elders and the pastor who retain a certain authority, but who, in general, seldom have a very precise or considered idea of the significance of the family in society, particularly of the Christian family.

Marriage is seldom a matter of careful thought to be entered into with conviction and the intention of bringing happiness to one's partner, in faithful and unselfish love. During adolescence, young people have great sexual freedom. No training having been given to them, they are initiated "naturally" very early and they consider this matter outside normal events; it is strange, hidden, something which is referred to by allusion or joke, often coarseness. Parents are ashamed to give their children sexual education and the church has never tried to help them. The ages of 14 to 21 are troubled times for our young people. They begin with a custom which has always been very widespread, although to-day conducted secretly—that of circumcision. Parents do not intervene and it is done without their knowledge. A boy, urged on by his fellows, finishes by believing he has an obligation to submit to this interference, which is represented as being of hygienic value! As all this happens outside the family, the child sees in it a mystery which is confined to "the bad things" and which does not fail to influence the boy strongly in detaching him from his family and their authority. Is this custom practised only in Eastern Polynesia? It will be interesting to know whether this is true of other parts of the Pacific.

Soon after, the young man and woman enter the "age of pleasure": *"taurearea"*. They find life good, with no obligations or responsibilities. They succumb to all temptations, they taste of all pleasures, they drink, gamble and go from diversion to diversion. When they find a partner of the other sex, they live together over the years. On coming of age, they become wise: *"paari"*, and finally think about regularising their position—the children help towards that; they have returned to their senses! Once married, there is no difficulty in joining a group of catechumens and several months later may be received into the Church as a *"membre d'eglise"* (Ekalesia), which is the first grade in the Christian community. The second is that of *"diacre"* (Diakono) and the summit of the hierarchy is the *"Diacre"*—the spokesman for the parish (*auha paroika*) who has a seat on the church council.

II

When one says that in our Polynesian isles there are no more pagans, it is true in the widest sense of the term. All the indigenous inhabitants are in effect attached to a religion, all were baptised in infancy (except the Adventists)—Protestants, Catholics, Mormons,

Kanites. There are no longer pagan ceremonies (except those laid on
for tourists) nor pagan altars retaining vestiges of their prestige, but
there are still many superstitions, and certain sorcerers who keep
them alive. One can say that of the whole indigenous population
to-day, 70%—80% are Protestant. But of this number, how many
Tahitians know what this membership signifies and try to live in
conformity with the Gospel? This will be a small enough proportion,
it must be said! The Evangelical Church, established many years
ago, suffered in the early days—and before it had reached spiritual
manhood—from the fierce attacks of the French Administration, for
whom all that was Protestant was English!, and also from the Catholic priests who wished to stamp out the Protestant heresy, often by
very tortuous means. (This desire is still the same to-day.) It was
not until 20 years after the English L.M.S. missionaries had left that
French pastors arrived in Tahiti, at the request of the Protestant
population. But for a long time they had to wrestle (and it is still
the same to-day) with an Administration always pro-Catholic and
ignorant of the true Tahitian character. In spite of all this, the
Tahitian Church has survived and represents a force and a hope
amongst this island people. It is continually assailed by contradictory influences which gain ready acceptance in a people still lovable
and simple. Propaganda and bids for their attention divide the
people and reduce the authority of the Church and its pastors. There
is only partial concern for the good of the people, but one's own
personal advantage counts much more. The influence of American
tourism, backed by influential people in Papeete, could very rapidly
and absolutely ruin the Polynesian people.

In the Church itself, law outweighs love, and obedience a free
decision. For this reason, Christian growth is much slower. Having
said that, and to return to our subject, let me make it clear that
without doubt there are families who wish to live by the Gospel.
There are many men and women who have lived through their "age
of pleasure" who are coming to understand little by little the idea
of a Christian family and have the wish to give their children training and evangelical instruction. But how often is this care associated
with false ideas, inherited from the legalistic past, spoiling the free
growth of life in the glorious liberty of the Children of God. Amongst
the families most closely connected with the church, children are
reared in strict discipline, which allows for little freedom or confidence, but which requires obedience. It is not unusual for children
to remain silent and even listless, lacking in curiosity, in the presence
of their parents—who require of them much work in the household
and even on the plantations. One sees children who attend Sunday
School very regularly—and who may have to walk several kilometres
there and back, and miss a meal to do so—but the parents do not
interest themselves in what the children are doing! The role of the
local church is recognized and people will willingly respond to the
calls of Pastor or Deacon, but it is rather out of a desire for a few

hours' company than in an attempt to profit from what is said. The children are taught morning and evening prayers, grace before meals and the Ten Commandments. There may be regular family worship, but somehow it lacks spontaneity, joy, depth. It always seems to be a duty! The Bible is read very willingly, but how little this reading enriches daily life!

It must be noted that a greater sense of responsibility in the family has arisen in the last 20 years ; a responsibility connected with schooling. In other days parents' responsibilities consisted mostly in sending children to school so that they could learn to read and write— something soon forgotten afterwards! After the development of the school system, it became easier to obtain remunerative posts, and education was seen as the door to a new life. Responsibility to one's children was then seen in the light of sending them to school so that they might one day find a good job in Papeete. In Christian families, this attitude is conspicuous, but rarely lasts beyond schooldays. Once left school, at between 11 and 14, a young man needs to find a job and many disappointments and failures follow. In Papeete the problem of juvenile delinquents is becoming very serious.

It is therefore urgent that the Church should understand its role as educator and that the local church give guidance, even if only in outline, to parents to help them in the Christian training of their children. Leaflets such as are printed by some churches could be the basis of fruitful discussion and suggest to us how to proceed.

In closing, I must speak of something very widespread and the source of much failure—the numerous separations, both before marriage and afterwards by divorce. It is not unusual to see at the Mairie in Papeete more notifications of divorce than publications of banns. Marriage, in the view of many, restricts a man's liberty, as do other laws and Administration edicts. One feels cramped by a law which ties one to one's partner! It is not unusual for a legal marriage to be followed very quickly by a request for divorce, after which the parties live together again! Very rarely do Tahitians understand the depth and reality of the marriage bond. They consider it a constraint imposed from outside. And any constraint makes them feel ill and want to change their minds! There is no logic in it. Because of this, we have in our local churches very few marriages between young people. Marriage is only undertaken to regularise, by the wish of both parties, a situation which has existed for several years. Such regularisation signifies that they have become men of standing, and gives a right to consideration and other advantages.

You can see how the true meaning of marriage escapes most people. But who shall cast the first stone at this island people, in view of the example from outside, which has scarcely helped to solve the problems of Christian living! Certainly in the local churches, the pastors are trying to have abnormal situations regularised and are doing their best to prevent divorce. The results, unfortunately, are not particularly satisfactory; without a change of heart, how can one change a man? An enormous effort is required to instruct, to educate, to lead our people in all these fields of Christian living— marriage, family, children, training, etc. But who will help us? Who will show the teachers how to recover the soul of a people? How will they know that only Christian Love can save our people, can save the world? Here at this Conference we look for counsel and enlightenment; we look also for a new indwelling of the Holy Spirit.

Summary

Because of the lack of precision concerning the true meaning of "family" and "marriage" even, in most cases, within the Church, we are far from having a way of life complying with the will of God.

One of the most important problems is the lack of responsibility and of consciousness of obligations for most of those who live together (whether married or not). We are, actually, in a no-man's land—between the old, more or less strict, but forgotten social customs, and the modern world with its individualistic and egoistical idea of the family. The Church must, without delay, acknowledge the seriousness of this problem both for social life and its own witness.

The lack of precision in the notion of family life and the avoidance of true responsibility—even within a Christian way of thought— prevent social life being based on solid foundations. The lack of Christian personalities is a serious handicap and gives rise to fear for the future. How can the Church help?

Doubtless "the family" exists in really Christian circles, but without sufficiently strict discipline and without realising what freedom and confidence really mean. Parents do not yet fully realise the meaning of training based on love. They do, however, realise the part that education and the Church can play, but are not yet sufficiently conscious of their own responsibility. They are not sufficiently firm in their Christian duties.

The growing influence of the modern world, which penetrates everywhere, contradicts the affirmation of the Gospel and leaves the Church in defeat. (For instance, the disastrous effect of American "tourism".) We must reaffirm our assurance in Christ and continue to be the witnesses of His will to salvation.

The Christian Family
Address by Consultant, Mrs M. G. Wyllie (Australia)

This may well be the most provocative topic of the Conference. It certainly is a subject which vitally concerns each one of us. We all began our lives in a family, most of us have married and have established a new family. We all have the ideal of Christian marriage and a Christian family before us.

What I want to do this evening is to open up the subject. I do not hope, nor would I presume, to provide solutions to the many problems and questions that face us, whether they be in family life in Australia or the Pacific. I will try to be as practical as possible. Because we can learn so much by making comparison (I find that that is why our informal conversations in this Conference are so stimulating and valuable), I will attempt to use illustrations from Australia alongside illustrations from various parts of the Pacific. And as I speak, I am conscious of the failure in my own Australian society to maintain a Christian pattern of marriage and the family.

I feel a certain amount of diffidence in speaking to you because I am well aware that it is not the custom in many societies represented here for women to speak on any subject. Of course, this is not a custom peculiar to the Pacific; it is only on rare occasions that a woman speaks in the courts and conferences of the Church in Australia. So, maybe my words will not reach you with the same authority as they would if spoken by a man. And this pleases me, because I do not wish to speak with authority, but with humility and, as far as possible, with understanding and love.

And lest you think that because it is a woman speaking to you on this subject, and a woman, Mrs. Mataafa, chairing this discussion group, that the topic of the Christian family is women's work and not men's work, let me stress at the beginning that this subject is equally important for Christian men and Christian women. The Christian family is built upon the personality and the integrity of both the husband and the wife.

I

In every society the family is the basic social unit. Kinship ties are close and deep in every community. Being a member of a family brings privileges and economic, social and spiritual obligations. The family can be and should be the greatest source of security in the life of the individual. It is within the family that the basic personality structure of the individual is laid down in the early formative months and years of childhood. I would suggest that family ties are stronger, more satisfying, more meaningful, and more exacting in the Pacific than in Australia where I come from. The institution of marriage on which the family is founded is everywhere a union of a man and a woman, recognised by custom and law and instituted with a socially sanctioned procedure. Marriage is normally expected to be stable and enduring because it is concerned with the fulfilment of the personality of the husband and wife and the procreation and rearing of children. Marriage is a social institution as well as a personal arrangement between two people. We of the Western countries must remember this, for some people in our societies tend to regard marriage as merely a matter of individual choice and individual responsibility. In any particular marriage, family groups are involved, and society as a whole is involved. Because of the basic nature of marriage and the family the Church is deeply involved too.

The pattern of marriage and the form of the family differ greatly from society to society. This Conference is made up of people from many different societies with different ways of life: e.g., we live in different kinds of houses and we eat different kinds of food, we speak different languages, each one of us is the product of our cultural background. We will not always agree in our ideas on sex, marriage and the family, e.g., we may not all agree on the manner in which wealth and property should be handed down in families, or even on what degree of kinship-relationship marriage should be forbidden. We will differ in our ideas of the public ceremonies required by our societies for the recognition of marriage—the exchange of gifts, the eating of a meal together in public, or the standing together and making vows in church and the signing of documents.

But we have at least two things in common:

(i) we have a real concern for the welfare of our families and for the stability of marriage in our own societies;

(ii) we are bound together by Christian faith and experience and we have a common task to discover the significance of the Christian faith for this important area of our life.

We can help one another by sharing our traditions, our problems, our successes and our failures.

II

In all parts of the world there is evidence that individuals and communities are concerned for the stability of marriage and the welfare of the family. "The Christian Family" is a subject which would appear on the Conference paper of most conferences in the world called to discuss the relevance of the Christian Gospel to twentieth century society. This concern is felt by Christian and non-Christian alike. Sociologists, politicians, the ordinary "man in the street", are interested. But the Christian has a special responsibility because Christian faith and the Christian ethic are concerned with the human relationships which are the foundation of marriage and the family.

The World Council of Churches and the International Missionary Council have encouraged discussion and publications on the Christian approach to marriage and the family. The study of African Marriage was the result of the difficulties met in the discussions on Christian marriage at the Tambaram Conference. More recently consultations have been held in Manila on "The Christian Family in Changing East Asia" and a consultation in the Caribbean.

The World Council's Department on the Co-operation of Men and Women has been increasingly concerned with the theological issues bearing on marriage and family problems.

In preparation for the Lambeth Conference in 1958, a committee within the Church of England prepared a report on *"The Family in Contemporary Society"*. It goes deeply into the theology of the family and marital relationships and also deals with the problem caused by the rapid rise in the rate of increase of the world's population. Contributions from U.S.A., Canada and the West Indies and Mauritius, India and the Middle East illustrate both the world-wide nature of the problems involved and the ways in which the Church is approaching them. We can learn much from the reports of these conferences.

From these reports of conferences from different parts of the world and from literature recently published, it is increasingly evident that the Church, each local church, is accepting its duty under the Holy Spirit, to study the local situation and so to order its teaching, its pastoral ministry, and its organisation that it can discover and do the will of God in relation to the family and society.

III

It is never easy to discuss sex, marriage and the family. These matters are bound up with strong emotion and sentiments, which are part of our personality structure. Our thinking about them has been largely fashioned for us by the traditions of our own societies and it is hard to think objectively about them. These are subjects which we find easier to discuss in our own language, rather than in the acquired languages of English and French. We all tend to believe that our pattern of marriage is the best and only reasonable pattern. When I talked with a friend about this topic, "The Christian Family" —a friend who knows the Australian scene well and who also knows and loves the Pacific—he said: "Realism and candour are needed in all discussions on this subject of marriage".

Realism and candour, sincerity and honesty, those words remained with me and I hope that they will characterise our discussions together. We all appreciate the sincerity and candour with which Mr. Raapoto has analysed the conditions in Tahiti. Many subjects will call for courageous thinking, such as the question of the attitude to chastity before marriage in societies where formerly this has not been the custom. I understand that there are many parts of the Pacific where promiscuity before marriage was accepted as the normal thing. Old customs and ideas do not change easily. Fashions in dress, changes in food habits, the use of new tools and techniques, are accepted much more easily and quickly than new ideals in sex relationships and family matters.

IV   *Rapid Social Change*

Social change is taking place in all societies—in the Pacific, in America, Europe, Africa and Asia. We in Europe, America and Australia have had a longer time to become adjusted to the social changes which have stemmed from the Industrial Revolution. But in some areas, as in the Pacific, we add the adjective "Rapid" to describe the speed with which these changes are taking place. Within our generation, or more exactly during and since the Second World

War, we have watched a social revolution taking place. The way of life of Pacific peoples is changing. For some, as in Suva, Apia and other big cities, the process is far advanced; in others, as in parts of Melanesia, in the Highlands of New Guinea, the forces of rapid change are only now becoming active.

When changes in many different aspects of life take place at once we sometimes speak of "disintegration" or "breaking up" of a people's way of life. This often brings disheartening confusion. It is necessary for us to understand how change in one part of a people's way of life can produce something unexpected in another part of their life.

I have been very interested in an article written about the introduction of steel axes to a tribe of Australian Aborigines in Northern Queensland. It seemed such a simple thing to offer this obvious labour saving device to a people whose only weapons were made of stone, wood and shell. But when the writer of the article traced the repercussions of that simple, kindly transaction through to changes in the marriage pattern, changes in the status system of the people and changes in their relations with neighbouring tribes, I realized how complex and involved the process of social change can be. It is not only steel axes, but a multitude of techniques, ideas, methods of government, changes in economic organization and a new and different religion that have been introduced into the Pacific. It is small wonder that there are resultant changes at the very centre of life—in the relationship between the sexes, in the pattern of marriage, and in the family group. And while I am speaking about the integration of all parts of a culture, it is interesting and important to see how this works in the other direction. The practice of chiefly polygamy in the Trobriand Islands has been retained after seventy years of Christian preaching. The chiefs have remained outside the Church, though they have at times supported it. Retained, because it is so closely integrated with social system. Polygamy is one important way in which the chiefly system is maintained and the integration of the society is safeguarded.

In some parts of the Pacific the impact of Western civilization in the last fifty years has been shattering. The other concepts of right and wrong have been confused, the sanctions which formerly governed morality and behaviour have been discarded and people have been left disturbed and confused, as Mr. Raapoto has mentioned. This is certainly true of attitudes to sex, to marriage and to attitudes within the family. This is important and it is significant for the study of "The Christian Family" because the family should be the source of security and integration for the development of the personality of the children within the family.

I would go so far as to say that no institution has been more affected by social crisis and change than the family. Marriage and the family are relationships so basic in their nature that there can hardly be any event in human society which does not influence them directly or indirectly. Because of this, this generation has been forced into a self-conscious examination of a complex institution which until now we have largely taken for granted. There is no society that is not deeply concerned.

May I speak for my own country? In Australia the traditions of the "Victorian" family have been challenged—by "Victorian", I mean the pattern and standards of fifty years ago. The family is smaller (2.2 children in our statistical family), the functions of the family are restricted, more mothers are working outside the home, the divorce rate is rising, the place of authority within the home is changing, a new ideal of partnership of husband and wife is emerging, teen-age sex behaviour is more sophisticated and less disciplined, i.e. the pattern of our Australian family life is changing. The Church and society in Australia are concerned, and perhaps the two main contributions that the Church has been able to make have been (i) the study of the Christian doctrine of sex and marriage, and (ii) the setting up of Marriage Guidance Centres, whose function is to educate and to counsel and to assist in saving marriages that are breaking up. Some of these changes Australia shares with the Pacific, but some are peculiar to Australia.

In the Pacific, the Church and society face the repercussions that arise for marriage and the family from this period of rapid social change. These will differ from country to country and are best known to the people of those countries, but there are some results that all will share. The preliminary reports that came from the various Churches in the different Pacific countries set out many problems that are being faced. May I mention some of them: the increase in wage-labour in place of the older communal labour ordered by the family, the breaking down of the extended or enlarged family, the growth of big towns, the changing status of women, the new place that she is taking in society as the result of Christian education, the increasing demand for freedom of choice of marriage mates, the rapid increase in population, the desirability or necessity for the civil registration of marriage. In the Pacific, as in Australia, the old pattern of marriage and the family has been challenged.

But there are some aspects of the older pattern in the Pacific which seem to us who come from outside to be more Christian than our pattern, e.g. the care of the aged, the widow and the orphan within the extended family; the assurance that marriage is available for all members of the community; and the concern and interest in the family groups involved in the stability of a marriage. These are some aspects of family life in the Pacific which shame our Western way of life.

And now another problem has come as a direct result of the introduction of modern medicine. In many parts of the Pacific 45% of the population is under 15 years of age. Against the background of this unprecedented increase in population in the present and the near future, the fundamental question of the Christian doctrine of the family assumes very great importance. The Christian responsibility for planned and responsible parenthood is becoming a matter of urgency.

The increase of population confronts parents with the question of family planning. These are problems fraught with moral and theological implications. The Churches must face the question realistically if they are to help parents make responsible Christian decisions.

I am sure that we all agree that the Church has a heavy responsibility in a country where there is rapid social change. The Church in the community should not be a passive witness to the process of change or merely a restraining or conservative influence but can and should be an active participant.

For example, the Church wherever it is, in Australia or Noumea or New Guinea, must be actively interested in the changes taking place in marriage and the family and in the quality of the married life and family life of its people. To do this, the Church will have to provide thorough training of its ministry and of lay men and women. By this I mean not only theological and Biblical training, but it must provide an understanding of the process of social change and also a training in marriage guidance, in Christian sex education and in family life and welfare.

V

Christian Teaching on Marriage and the Family

The report of the Caribbean consultation asked for a "careful and precise formulation of the Christian doctrine of Marriage". I can well imagine that the Group on "The Christian Family" will begin at this point. I am impressed with the amount of work that has been done on this subject in the last five years. Christians know that for them every development, every change in social institutions poses questions which can ultimately be answered only theologically. The question must always be asked: "What is the purpose of God for this vital area of our life? What is the purpose and will of God for marriage and the family?". But the fact is that most of the published work on the theology of marriage and the family has come from European thinkers. This is surely one of the fields of life and thought where the Church is waiting for the insights and conclusions of Christians in Asia, Africa and the Pacific. We should not too readily conclude that the Western family pattern holds the only solution. I remember reading of the frustration and despair of the African Christians as they left the Tambaram Conference, because they felt that the Christians in other parts of the world did not understand the desperate problems which African Christians must face. It is unnecessary and unrealistic to-day to press the Christian Gospel into the mould of the Western world. It is imperative to find the essential Christian Gospel for East and West, for Africa and the Pacific. The Rev. D. Kitagawa of Japan has recently written of the impact of the Christian Gospel of marriage and the family in Japan, under the title *"Freedom of marriage and its relations to Family Patterns—the Christian viewpoint"*. Some African Christians are writing of the agonies of their countrymen in working out a theology of Christian marriage, particularly in relation to polygamy.

How easy it would be if we could go to the Bible and find there a blue-print of Christian marriage and the family. Jesus gave very little specific teaching on marriage and the family. There are many other social issues, e.g. pacifism, slavery, capitalism, on which He gave little specific teaching. The foundation of a Christian Doctrine of marriage and the answers to our many questions must be sought in the life and teaching and spirit of Jesus, and they must be sought in relation to the present social situation. We must seek a contemporary model for the Christian family and that will need hard and continuous thinking. This is true for Australia and for the Pacific.

In our study of the Bible, in our search for a Christian doctrine of marriage, there are some important things to remember.

(i) That the Old Testament shows us a progressive revelation of God and His purpose for mankind. It shows us the development of ideas and institutions. The Hebrew people lived a long time ago and their pattern of marriage and the family frequently does not fit into the 1961 Christian picture. Thus we find David and Solomon with many wives and we find easy forms of divorce. When we come to the prophets and the Song of Solomon we find a different and a higher ideal.

(ii) In the New Testament, while Jesus answered only two questions on marriage and divorce, He did give us ultimate truths about human relationships generally, and on the ultimate worth of individual human personality.

(iii) St. Paul, when he writes on marriage in his letters, is not easy to understand. We must accept a change or development in his thinking. From an advocacy of celibacy in his earlier writings, he moves in the later letters to the wonderful analogy of the Church as the Bride of Christ. Biblical scholars tell us that his ideas changed as he realised that the *parousia* was not necessarily imminent. He realized that the begetting of children and Christian family life were part of the continuing purpose of God.

The Bible does not deal explicitly and directly with the questions which the modern Church must ask regarding men and women relationships. It deals with the will of God against the background of the social situations in which its several books are written. We cannot hope to find the way at the cross roads by asking what the guide book says on this particular point. When we read the Bible we must look for the heart of the matter instead of grasping single texts and words. This is particularly necessary in working out the Christian basis of marriage and the family.

It seems to me that there are three sources which we can use in our search for the Christian Doctrine of Marriage and the Family— the Bible, the ritual and services of marriage of the various churches, and the experience, the thinking and writing of Christian scholars and disciples. I have spoken already about the Bible. Marriage ritual and services differ from denomination to denomination and from century to century. But they enshrine the sacred tradition of the Church. Some branches of the Christian Church regard marriage as a Sacrament, others do not. Marriage ritual, by its very nature is precious and conservative. But I often wish that the churches could simplify and clarify many of the phrases in the Marriage Service and give them the rich meaning that should belong to them. This becomes a matter of urgency as the Marriage Service is used for the first time in churches of the Pacific. These services of marriage set out the purpose of Christian marriage. The phrases used differ from church to church, but could they perhaps be summarized in this way? Marriage is for—

(1) the procreation of children;

(2) the fulfilment of the life and personality of the man and the woman. "The mutual help and comfort, the one ought to have of the other."

(3) the care and nurture of the family. "That children may be brought up in the fear and admonition of the Lord."

I will try to summarise what seem to me to be the basic Christian beliefs on which we can work in our search for a "careful and precise formulation of the Christian Doctrine of Marriage":

(a) Christians believe that sex, in itself, is good and part of the purpose of God; the process of human reproduction is regarded as being invested with a special and responsible dignity. Sex is the most creative urge that we possess; it is essentially valuable and wholesome.

(b) The New Testament points to two analogies or similarities or word pictures which show a high regard for and give responsibility to Christian marriage and the family.

(i) The comparison of the union of Christ and the Church and the marriage union of a man and a woman described in the letter to the Ephesians.

(ii) The concept of the Divine Fatherhood and the parent-child relationship.

(c) The Gospels, e.g. Matthew ch. V, insist upon the ultimate worth of human personality and demand respect for individuals as sons and daughters of God. This Christian teaching has great importance for the intimate and personal relationship within marriage, for attitudes of youth before marriage, and for the parent-child relationship.

---

1. To change the world is a tremendous task, but one way in which we can start straight away is by making our homes fit places for our children to grow up in. There is no way in which we can more successfully work for the new and better world we all long and

pray for than by increasing the number of happy Christian marriages.
2. All families that are true and noble centre in marriage. A man
and woman come together in love and pledge devotion to each other
and so a family is founded, and the quality of that family is deter-
mined by the unfolding love between that man and woman. There
is much greater hope of building well-integrated individual personalities within the family if the marital relationship of the parents is
happy and well adjusted and based on Christian faith and practice.
3. Our homes should be places where we can develop that type of
man and woman that loves the good, the just, the honest, the true
and the beautiful qualities of life.

Conclusion

This Conference I hope will be a summons to the Churches in these
lovely islands to embark on the long and difficult search for the
Christian pattern of marriage and the family. In this search the
mistakes, the discoveries and the traditions of the Older Churches
must never be accepted as a substitute for the prayer, the Bible
study and the study of your own changing way of life and your own
particular social background. It is *in* the Pacific and *for* the Pacific
that you will ultimately discover the will of God for marriage and
the family.

This prayer and this study can be most effectively carried out as a
co-operative effort on the part of Christian men and Christian women
together. This co-operation of men and women in thinking through
the Christian basis of marriage and the family will in itself be an
adventure in Christian discipleship. This task will not be easy but it
must not be avoided or neglected, for we believe as Christians that
the future rests with the family and the children. In this task may I
assure you that the Churches which we visitors to the Pacific represent
will follow you with our prayers and our love.

Bible Study on the Letter to the Galatians

Note: The following are summaries, provided by the Rev. Hans-Ruedi Weber, of the eight studies which he led at the Conference. Each was followed by group study in small groups; it is possible only to give the tasks assigned for the work of the groups. This material therefore cannot convey either the vividness of the exposition or the searching character of the group study. It is hoped, however, that to those present at the Conference it may recall this most enriching experience and to those who were not present it may convey some impression of this central part of the Conference's work, without which the rest cannot be seen in its true setting. Any group in the churches in the Pacific which used the exposition and engaged in the group work suggested would find it a rewarding undertaking and would thereby be sharing in the life of the Conference.—Editor.

Study I
PAUL'S OWN SUMMARY

Paul was no stranger to the Galatians. On the first missionary journey he and Barnabas had visited the Southern part of the Roman province of Galatia (Acts 13 and 14). "A door of faith was opened" (Acts 14:27), and Paul testifies to his readers that they "were running well" (Galatians 5:7).

But then something terrible happened. Some preachers had come to Galatia claiming that they alone could bring the true Gospel (1:6). Apparently they were Jews who had become Christians, but who considered the Christian Church still to be a part of the Jewish congregation. They claimed, therefore, that they were completing the missionary work Paul had begun, and they did so by requesting the Christians in Galatia to live according to the law of Moses. For they said (and this was the gist of their message) that only through circumcision and a life according to the Mosaic law can one really belong to Abraham, the father of the holy people of God. And only by becoming in this way "the sons of Abraham" is it possible to become the heirs of the promises made to Abraham and his people (3:6f). In particular, circumcision (5:2f) and the keeping of the Jewish periods of fasting (4:10) were essential to receive salvation. At the same time these Jewish-Christian preachers undermined the authority of the apostle Paul; they said he was only an apostle of minor importance who worked under the authority of the persons who really mattered, namely the "pillars" in Jerusalem (1:1, 12; 2:2, 6, 9). In addition, they probably cast suspicion on Paul's own character and behaviour (1:10; 5:11). This "new gospel" apparently "bewitched" the young congregations in Galatia to such an extent that they were in danger of becoming a Jewish Christian sect which considered the keeping of the law as a new way of salvation (1:6; 3:1f).

In such a situation everything was at stake, not only Paul's whole life-work, not only the salvation of the Christian congregations in Galatia, but also Christ and his whole Church in all ages and continents. Should this Church be enslaved in the old forms of Judaism? Paul considered it therefore timely to pose the question of truth without any compromise and false softness. He dictated the sharpest and most penetrating epistle of his missionary struggle. And he was so carried away by his concern that at the end of the letter he put not only his personal signature, but wrote with his own hand his own summary (6:11-18).

It is quite probable that, when opening the letter, the eyes of the Galatians fell first on this postscript in Paul's own hand-writing, and that the Galatians read the postscript first. We are therefore beginning our study of Galatians with the examination of this postscript.

For Group Work:

(1) Which, in your opinion, were for Paul and the Galatians the three key terms in Paul's own summary in 6:11-18?

(2) Why were these terms central to Paul and the Galatians?

(3) How are these terms usually translated in your own language or paraphrased in modern colloquial terms?

(4) Are the issues raised by these terms relevant to the Church situation in the Pacific to-day?

Study II
BAPTIZED INTO CHRIST

When Paul in the course of his plea to the Galatians makes clear the great lines of God's history of salvation, he constantly tells them that they are personally involved in this drama. Either they play the role of God's sons in it, or else they are being used as puppets by the powers and principalities of this world. How did the life of the Galatians become so intimately involved in the history of salvation? Where did that amazing identification with the cross of Christ happen, about which Paul speaks in 2:20?

Paul did not speak here about his individual mystical experiences; he described the general Christian condition: "We as Christians have been crucified". This assertion must be seen in the context of Paul's understanding of baptism: cp. 3:27 and Romans 6:3-11; Colossians 2:12. Baptism for Paul was in the first place our death sentence. In baptism we are drawn into the death of Christ (see study IV on the Law), so that we may receive new life. Paul did not say that everybody who is baptized is automatically changed. But for him, the Galatians and the early Christians the whole series of events beginning with hearing the Gospel and conversion was crystallized in the act of baptism. And although in his letter to the Galatians Paul spoke only once explicitly about baptism (3:27), many other passages must be seen in relation to that decisive event in the life of the Christians in Galatia: cf. 1:4; 2:20; 3:1, 26-28; 5:24; 6:14, 17.

The early Church expressed Paul's understanding of baptism in the right way when it included the following elements in its baptismal liturgy: the renouncement of the devil; the unction of exorcism; the threefold immersion combined with the confession of God, Father, Son and Holy Spirit (an old Christian baptistry on the island of Rhodes is cut in the rock in the form of a large cross filled with water: here the converts were in a literal sense identified with the cross); the putting on of white garments; the new unction which meant the "ordination" of a new member into the participation in Christ's priestly, prophetic and royal ministry.

For Group Work:

(1) How is Paul's understanding of baptism as our death with Christ and our incorporation into the drama of salvation being expressed in the baptismal teaching, liturgy and ceremonial in your Church?

(2) If Paul's understanding of baptism is not sufficiently seen in your Church, suggest ways in which it could be better expressed in words and gestures which are both true to Paul's teaching and meaningful to the people in the Pacific.

Study III
SONS OF ABRAHAM

Abraham is a central figure in the letter to the Galatians. Not Abraham as the Judaizing party among the Galatians saw him, namely the national religious hero of the Jewish people, but Abraham as Paul saw him in Christ, namely, the typical and exemplary "nomad of faith" who dared to trust God's promises and therefore became God's agent of redemption (cp. Galatians 3:6-29; 4:22-31). Paul's refutation of the exegesis of the Judaizers by his own exegesis is not always clear and conclusive for us to-day. But Paul himself quoted that Old Testament passage (Genesis 12:1-3) which expresses in a few words the very centre of the character and mission of Abraham.

According to Genesis 12:1, 2 the following things make Abraham the typical incorporation of the total Israel and the Church: He is the man to whom God speaks, who has been seen, elected and called by God. He is the man who listens to God, obeys His will and is thereby made free from all earthly links. He is the man to whom God addresses His promises and who sets all his trust in these promises. The two parts of the third verse of that passage show us Abraham's mission: on the one hand he is to be the testing point for the nations; through him the nations are brought into a crisis. And on the other hand Abraham is to become a source of blessing for all.

For Group Work:

As "sons of Abraham" church members have a double task: (a) On the one hand the presence of the Church among a people must bring that people to decide for or against God; (b) on the other hand the Church must become a source of blessing for all.

(1) How can we do the one task without neglecting the other?

(2) Which of these tasks do our churches fulfil or neglect to-day?

Study IV

UNDER THE LAW

We find ourselves in a vexing dilemma: the law brings curse with it. Yet we cannot live without the law, for this would lead us into chaos. What does Paul teach us about the law, about which he spoke no less than twenty-seven times in his letter to the Galatians? Paul made seven assertions:

(1) The law, to him, was not just a set of human regulations, but God's codified will. Paul used the term "law" both for the Mosaic law (consisting of 248 positive and 365 prohibitive commandments) and for the whole story of God acting through His people as it is told to us in the Pentateuch, the first five books of the Bible. The law is the total will of God as it is revealed and written in the Old Testament.

(2) But this law was not the primary thing in the covenant between God and His people, as was maintained by the Judaizers. The primary thing was God's promise. The old covenant was not in the first place a legal covenant but a covenant of promise (3:8-20; 4:21-31).

(3) The law was for Israel an instrument of malediction and curse (3:10-13).

(4) It functioned also as a custodian until the coming of Christ (3:23-25; 4:1-3). This did not mean that by the law Israel was gradually educated into the maturity of faith. But the law kept Israel in contact with God because it gave the sin of Israel reality and led it therefore to its death sentence at the cross.

(5) At the cross the law came to its end and fulfilment: there Christ took all our disobedience to the revealed will of God upon Himself and was cursed for our sake (3:13). At the cross we were condemned to death (and in this death sentence also justified!). The only thing for us to do now is to accept this condemnation which is shown to us in our baptism into Christ. Paul's "no" to the law is therefore grounded in God's "no" to man at the cross.

(6) At the cross not only has sinful man been condemned and annihilated, but also the law itself which—against the original purpose God will for it—had become an instrument by which religious man could glorify himself before God apart from Christ. Law had indeed become an instrument of "the elemental spirits of the universe" (4:2-3). But now the law as a way of salvation has been done away with.

(7) In the new covenant the content of law remains the same: it is the revealed will of God which must be obeyed by God's people. But "the law of Christ" (6:2) is now seen in the context of our

freedom in Christ (5: 6, 13ff) and is brought in relation to the fruit
of the Spirit (5:16-23). The law of Christ keeps the people of the
new covenant in fidelity to the grace received in Christ.

For Group Work:

Church discipline is necessary.
In the light of Paul's understanding of the law evaluate the practice of discipline in your Church.

Study V

THE CROSS OF CHRIST

Paul reminded his readers not only of the great events in the history
of the old covenant between God and Israel, he pointed them above
all to the centre of the history of salvation: the cross and redemption. In this sense Galatians 4:3-7 is the dogmatic centre of the
letter.

Verse 3 reminds us of our heathen past, and it is very revealing for
us and shocking for the Jewish Christians that Paul combined in the
"we" converted Jews and heathen alike who, whether they were under
the law or not, had become puppets of "the elemental spirits of the
universe".

But then God took the new and decisive initiative: He sent forth
His Son (v. 4). God's children, Jews and heathens alike, had lost
their rights as children. They were alienated from God. But
through His self-offering at the cross Jesus Christ died for them and
with them, so that in this same event those condemned to death could
be adopted as sons. Through this sovereign act of adoption out of
pure grace the promises made to Abraham were renewed and we
were given a new life. In this same decisive intervention God then
sent forth the Spirit (v. 6). Jesus used the same verb when later
He sent out His disciples. The mission of the Church is thus
embedded in God's mission through His Son by which the Church
was created. And the first act of our participation in this mission is
prayer, the confident response of the adopted children to their
Father.

For Group Work:

It is possible that Galatians 4:3-7 contains old Christian catechetical formulae. Write therefore a catechism on "The Good News"—
in simple, contemporary language which could be understood by
non-Christians in the Pacific—by answering the four following questions on the basis of Galatians 4:3-7.

(1) What is the heart of the good news which we believe?
(2) What does this good news tell us about our life in the time
before we knew Christ?
(3) What does this good news tell us about our life now that we
have come to know Christ?
(4) Which beliefs held in my Church must therefore be rejected?

Study VI
FAITH IN GOD WHO JUSTIFIES

When Martin Luther studied and explained Paul's letters to the Romans and the Galatians he discovered something which made history. In accordance with the whole scholastic theology of the Middle Ages, he had understood the term "the righteousness of God" in the sense that God becomes righteous by punishing the sinners. But Luther now learned from Paul that the righteousness of God must be understood in the sense that God makes us righteous. And instead of being paralyzed by fear and hatred in the presence of a punishing God, the Reformer began now to discover the power of the faith in a God who justifies.

Paul spoke about this faith in 5:5-6. Belief comes from the Spirit who is the provisional help given to the militant and expectant Church. And this belief based on the past event of the cross and looking forward with hope to the future event of the judgment has a special "radiation" in the present time: it is a "faith expressing itself in love".

The life lived by the Spirit and by faith is not just a higher level of life we reach after having lived under the law. It is something quite new, a "new creation" (6:15). This newness does not mean that man is morally made better or that he has been magically transformed. It means that *according to the judgment of God* man has been condemned to death and then been created anew. The fundamental change has happened in God's heart, which for Hebrew thinking is the measure of all things. Faith in God who justifies is the adventure of believing that in God's judgment I am a new creation.

For Group Work:

(1) What is, according to Galatians 4:8-10 and 5:4-6, the real difference between a Christian and a non-Christian? Make a list of the marks of a Christian and non-Christian life.

(2) According to these measures, how Christian are we Christians in the Pacific?

Study VII
WALK BY THE SPIRIT!

Paul did not exhort the Galatians and us to become what they and we should be. Christian life is not a constant race after an ideal, and the term "should" must be erased from Christian language. Paul's exhortation is that we become what we are. We have already the new life. We can sometimes sit down, smile and enjoy ourselves, dance and sing. We need not be "beastly serious", all the time worrying about the degree of sanctity we have or have not yet achieved.

Become what you are! "Because we live in the Spirit, march (make your decisions from day to day in your every-day life, your job, family and nation) in the Spirit" (5:25). This exhortation concludes Paul's discussion about the polarity between "flesh" and "Spirit" in 5:16-25. "Flesh" is total man with body and mind but without the guidance of the Spirit and therefore a prey to all temptations, man abandoned to himself. The list of the "works of the flesh" shows that most of these works are social vices, that besides the sexual vices there are also equally serious religious vices; we can have a "fleshy" religion in our churches. The "harvest of the spirit"—love, joy, peace, patience, etc.—is not something we do, but something which is a spontaneous manifestation, a "radiation" of the new life we have in Christ (cp. Matthew 25:31-40). As soon as love, joy, etc. are a "work" instead of being the "fruit" of our new life, they become self-conscious love and joy which are very ugly things, belonging more to the realm of "flesh" than of "Spirit".

The basis of Paul's exhortation is the assertion in verse 24: "Those who belong to Christ Jesus have crucified the flesh with its passions and desires". The Christian answer to the flesh and its desires is not a life regulated and safeguarded by a whole set of "must" and "must not", of "tabus" and obligations. Nor is it a life from which all temptations have carefully been removed. The Christian answer to the flesh is the fact of crucifixion: we have at our baptism actively and consciously accepted our death sentence and condemnation. The source of the works of the flesh, the flesh itself, *is* dead. We *are* a new creation, therefore we must manifest what we are.

For Group Work:

In Galatians 5:16-25 Paul probably again freely quoted catechetical material which was used in Christian teaching. Continue therefore to write a catechism in simple, contemporary language which can be understood by non-Christians in the Pacific to-day, adding a chapter on "The New Life". Answer the following three questions on the basis of Galatians 5:16-25:

(1) What is the basis of our new life in Christ?

(2) What must therefore be erased out of my life and the life of my Church?

(3) How does the new life manifest itself?

Study VIII
CALLED TO FREEDOM

When Paul dictated his letter to the Galatians his first concern was to re-establish his apostolic authority so that the Galatians really would listen to his gospel of the grace of God (chapters 1 and 2). He then explained this gospel again and confirmed it with texts from the Old Testament (chapters 3 and 4). On the basis of this he finally came to his central plea: "For freedom Christ has freed us; stand fast therefore, and do not submit again to a yoke of slavery" (5:1). This central plea to the Galatians to recover their freedom in bondage to Christ gives us many important hints with regard to the right attitude towards our Christian heritage and our non-Christian environment:

(1) We are free in Christ, that means (a) free from everything and everybody, because we are in bondage to Christ; (b) free for love and therefore servants to all (5:1 ; 5:13-14).

(2) Jesus Christ who redeemed and freed us at the cross is the Messiah of Israel. Our freedom in bondage to Christ inserts us into the true Israel and its history of salvation. Therefore our freedom in Christ does not imply freedom from the Bible (Old and New Testament), but it frees us for a right understanding of the Bible. Because Christ is, on the one hand, the fulfilment of the law, our freedom in Christ does not give us liberty no longer to obey our Lord. Yet because, on the other hand, Christ is the condemnation of the law, our freedom in Christ frees us from the tyranny of non-Christian and Christian customs.

(3) While there is an inner continuity between the Jewish-Christian heritage and our Christian faith to-day, there is no such point of contact and continuity between our heathen environment and our Christian faith. Therefore we must be "delivered from the present evil age" (1:4), therefore Abraham, the nomad of faith, becomes the "type" of the Church (3:6f), therefore we must be crucified and created anew. In this sense we are free from all customs, laws, and regulations, none of which any longer carry any weight in the judgment of God (and remember: this, the judgment of God, is for a biblically trained mind the ultimate norm and authority!). However, this radical freedom from our environment makes us also free *for* our environment. Christ came *into* the world, "born of a woman, born under the law" (4: 4). Our freedom in Christ immediately means also to become free for the world, for our environment with all its customs. Freedom from the world and solidarity with the world are therefore not mutually exclusive in Christ. But as soon as something in that environment begins to usurp the place of Christ's redeeming work at the cross, we must, together with Paul, say a radical "no". In all other cases, however, the love for which we are liberated compels us to "bear one another's burdens" (6:2) and to be in solidarity with the world. The aim of this Christian solidarity is none other than the purpose of Christ's solidarity with men: ". . . so that he may redeem" (4:5).

For Group Work:

Express Paul's message about our freedom in bondage to Christ by a simple mime:

How would you express with a position or movement of your body:

(1) Paul's understanding of man in the bondage of his "flesh", under the law and the "elemental spirits of the universe"?

(2) Paul's understanding of the process of liberation?

(3) Paul's understanding of man believing in God who justifies, walking by the Spirit and being freed in his bondage to Christ?

Reports of Commissions

The Conference worked through five Commissions, on
- A. The Ministry.
- B. The Unfinished Task of Evangelism.
- C. The Relevance of the Gospel to Changing Conditions of Life in the Pacific.
- D. The Place of Young People in the Life of the Church.
- E. The Christian Family.

The *reports* of these commissions were discussed in the plenary sessions and, after some amendment, were received by the Conference. They are here given in the form in which they were so received. By "received" is meant that the Conference approved the general lines of the reports and commended them to the consideration of the churches and missions it represented, but is not committed to every detail in them or to their precise form of words.

A number of *resolutions* arose from the reports of the commissions, and after discussion and amendment were adopted by the Conference. These are included at the end of the report of the commission to which they are related. They represent actions of the Conference itself.

Several *general resolutions* of the Conference, including its important decisions on Church relationships in the Pacific, and on the continuance of the work of the Conference, will be found on pp. 99-102. —Editor.

Report of Commission A: The Ministry

The immense variety of conditions in the Pacific area makes it impossible for the Commission to make detailed recommendations. In the limited time available for the exchange of experience from widely differing situations, the following matters were briefly considered.

1. *Recruitment.* In general the tendency in the past in many areas has been that only older men of proved experience were selected for ordination. This has been valuable in providing for the needs of stable societies with a rural economy. It is, however, dangerous when conditions are changing and the Church is required to face new demands. The general trend in the churches is now to seek younger men who can be given a thorough training and who can serve for a long period. This trend must be strengthened, but without losing the great values in the older system.

There is also reported a changing emphasis in regard to the call of the minister. At an earlier stage it has been common for the church or mission authorities to call a man to ordination; now more stress is laid upon the inward sense of call of the individual. Clearly both elements have a proper place, both the call of God to the individual, and the action of the Holy Spirit in moving the Church to call a man (see Acts 13:1-3). The one should not be emphasised exclusively as over against the other.

2. *Support.* In very many parts of the area the ordained ministry is normally a part-time occupation which depends upon the support of a second occupation—teaching, agricultural work, or some other. This system has many advantages: it brings the minister into intimate relationship with his people; it provides a widely-spread ministry throughout large populations which could probably never have been effectively shepherded in any other way. But there is evidence that the system is breaking down in many places. Changing economic conditions make it increasingly difficult for ministers in some areas to live on the resources available to them. There are complaints that adequate teaching and pastoral care cannot be given by part-time pastors. In some cases ministers are suffering severely, and in many areas it is reported that men of sufficient education cannot be recruited for the ministry under the present conditions. We consider that the churches must attend, as a matter of urgency, to the economic conditions of the ministry. On the other hand, there are situations in which the part-time ministry may be a most valuable part of the whole pattern of ministry.

3. *Relation of the Minister to the Social Organization of the Community.* In this respect also there is a vast variety of situations. In some places the minister works in intimate relation with the established chiefly authority. In some places there have been conflicts of authority between ministers and chiefs. In some primitive areas the ministry appears to the people to be part of a powerful mission organization which is parallel to and comparable with the organization of Government. Clearly these problems must be answered in different ways in different areas. There is need for the Church in every place to prove itself both a blessing to the whole community, and also a place where men are called to acknowledge a kind of authority quite distinct from that of chief or government. This will not be proved if, for example, the minister is able to resist the authority of the chief only because he has behind him the stronger authority of the mission. It will be proved only when there are in the Church prophetic voices which call men to listen to the voice of God and to obey an authority which has no worldly power, but is the authority of the crucified Servant of God.

4. *The nature and function of the ministry.* The discussion of this subject has shown that there is a vast variety in the ways in which the special work of the ministry is understood as distinguished from the ministry in which all Christians share. There is great diversity in the ways in which ministerial duties are defined. We have the impression that in some cases there is a danger that the ministry may be understood as a certain grade provided for those of the highest educational and moral attainments, rather than in a way which is based upon Biblical teaching. We suggest that there is need in all

the churches for careful study, in the light of the Bible, of such questions as the following:
  (a) What is done in ordination?
  (b) What is a minister?
  (c) How is his function different from that of other Christians?
  (d) How is his work related to the life of the congregation?
  (e) The ordained ministry as part of the total ministry of the whole Church.

5. *Training for the ministry.* Discussion on this subject revealed a unanimous desire to raise the standard of theological training in all parts of the Pacific area. It is the opinion of this Commission that this could be best achieved by:
  (i) co-operation of the churches in the establishment of a central federated theological school to which selected graduates from our present schools can proceed for further training, provided that
        (a) a higher academic level is established, and
        (b) it offers the training relevant to the needs of the Pacific churches.
  (ii) urging the churches to do all within their power to raise the standard of training in the existing denominational colleges.

RESOLUTIONS
1. That this Conference recommends that occasional papers be prepared, by the participating churches, on the subjects listed in Section 4 of this Report, for circulation to and consideration by the churches sharing in the Conference.
2. That this Conference recommends the establishment of a Central Theological College in the South Pacific area, as outlined in Section 5 of this Report, and refers this matter to the forthcoming Consultation of the Theological Education Fund.

Report of Commission B:
The Unfinished Evangelistic Task

I. BASIS OF EVANGELISM

Evangelism is the communication to men of the Good News that, in Jesus Christ, God has acted in love to deliver man from the kingdom of darkness, and transfer him into the kingdom of His beloved Son.

In this task of evangelism, Jesus Christ Himself is the Evangelist. He calls His whole Church to share this ministry with Him. Every Christian must play his part, but to some will be given special gifts for evangelism.

Because of the limits of time, our discussions were primarily concerned with evangelism in its more restricted sense of offering Christ to those who do not know Him, both outside and within the life of the Church.

We realize, however, that the task of evangelism is wider and must include confronting the institutions of society with the Gospel of Jesus Christ.

Evangelism must always have a note of urgency. It is always concerned with "now".

II. SETTING FOR EVANGELISM

There are, we believe, five special spheres of evangelism to which Christ calls the Church in the Pacific:

1. Sharing in the task of taking the Good News "to the ends of the earth";
2. Exact statistics are not available, but there may well be one million Pacific island people (in New Guinea, the Solomons, New Hebrides and Micronesia) to whom the Gospel has not yet been preached;
3. There are Asian communities which are an integral part of Pacific life—200,000 Indians in Fiji, groups of Chinese scattered throughout the Pacific, 5,000 Javanese in New Caledonia, and a small Indonesian community in New Guinea. Though there are some Christians amongst them, the great majority of these people belong to the great non-Christian religions, and are entitled to know the Good News of Jesus Christ;
4. There is a confused group of "new pagans" arising in all territories—mostly young people whose faith in the Faith of their fathers has been shaken by travel, advanced education or contact with a secular way of life;
5. There is an urgent need to lead members of our Pacific churches into a fuller understanding of the Christian Gospel —"evangelism in depth".

III. LOOKING FORWARD

Members of this Commission have represented a wide range of Church life, but we realize we have by no means received an exhaustive report on the whole Pacific area. We make the following observations in the light of our discussions:

1. *The Church's "Evangelistic Dimension"*. If we are to be faithful in carrying out this evangelistic task, it is imperative that the "evangelistic dimension" of the Pacific Church be developed. How this may be done is a matter for the Church to determine in each area, after prayerful examination of its life.

We suggest that some help may be found from the study of the following:

   (a) the work of the Anglican Franciscan order in New Guinea;
   (b) the plans of the Church in Dutch New Guinea for the building up of the life of the congregation (see appendix C);
   (c) the experience of "house churches" in many areas. This may be of special relevance to our growing urban areas, and to work among Asian peoples;

(d) the system of "class leaders" who have pastoral responsibility for a small group of fellow Christians.

2. *Evangelism among Pacific Peoples.* As the Church faces its task of preaching the Gospel to non-Christian island people, especially in the Western Pacific, we suggest that insights may be gained from:

(a) the work of the indigenous Melanesian Brotherhood (see appendix B);

(b) the work of ecumenical teams in Dutch New Guinea. We would look forward to the creation of ecumenical teams, made up largely (perhaps) of members from widely scattered Pacific churches.

3. *Witness to others.* We regret that we have not had time to consider the responsibility of offering Christ to *our Asian brethren* in the Pacific. It is clear to us, however, that this is a task in which the Asian Church, through the East Asia Christian Conference, could help us much, both by consultation and also by the sending of Christian workers.

There are many *British, American and French* residents in Pacific territories whose lives have become increasingly secular. The witness and friendship of Pacific peoples may well be the means God will use to draw them back into the household of faith.

4. *The Gospel in Society.* In addition to this, we would press upon the Church in the Pacific the need to develop Bible Study and other study groups, particularly for the rising class of intellectuals in whose hands there will be increasing responsibility, and who urgently need to understand the relevance of the Gospel in a time of rapid social change. This is an important part of our evangelistic task.

5. *To the ends of the earth.* We wish to express our conviction, too, that the whole Church is called to proclaim the Gospel to the ends of the earth—not merely to the ends of the Pacific. The Gospel has permeated the life of so many of our island territories that the Pacific has become a "homeland of the Church". As such, it has a special responsibility for world evangelism.

The Church in every territory must face seriously her responsibility to send evangelists to work with the Church in other countries—in Europe (which is the "end of the earth" for us), in Asia, or in Africa, as well as other Pacific territories.

Many Pacific people are "on the move" in these days—their destination may be other island territories or much further afield—for work, study, or holidays. This "dispersion" could contribute to the renewal of the Church in the countries they visit—if their own Church has prepared them for the opportunities (and shocks) their travel will present to them.

IV. GENERAL RECOMMENDATIONS

1. We call the Church to a careful study of the use of radio, films, literature and drama—including dances and other Pacific art forms which may well be very valuable aids to evangelism.

We recommend close consultation with the All Africa Church Conference and the East Asia Christian Conference in these matters.

2. We suggest that there is room for a careful study of the distinction between evangelism and proselytism. The W.C.C./ I.M.C. paper on "Christian Witness, Proselytism and Religious Liberty" could provide a starting point for this.

3. We believe that the establishment of Lay Training Institutes, perhaps in association with our theological colleges, could do much to prepare the Church more effectively to witness to the truth of the Gospel in society.

In conclusion, while we have found our discussions very profitable, they have convinced us that there is need for a fuller study of the Pacific churches' unfinished evangelistic task, and of ways in which the whole Pacific Church may share in taking the Gospel to the ends of the earth.

RESOLUTIONS

1. The Commission heard with great interest a statement (see Appendix A) from the Rev. Ardi Soejatno, of five ways in which the East Asia Christian Conference and the Pacific Churches could co-operate in carrying out their unfinished evangelistic task. The Conference RESOLVED:

that we accept this statement with gratitude, append it to this Report for the information of the churches, and request the Continuation Committee of this Conference to consider ways of taking up its suggestions.

APPENDIX 'A'

Statement made by the Rev. Ardi Soejatno (Fraternal Representative of the East Asia Christian Conference) on co-operation with the East Asia Christian Conference

Expressing our deep gratitude for and appreciation of the privilege of participating in this Conference of Churches and Missions in the Pacific, we, as fraternal delegates from the E.A.C.C., desire to

1. seek the help and co-operation of the Church in the Pacific for some of our churches in East Asia to receive appropriate Christian workers from the Pacific, as may be discussed and followed up in detail in the future according to needs and opportunities;

2. share the Christian facilities at the disposal of the Churches in Asia, limited as they are, to provide opportunities of training to members of the Pacific churches;

3. where needed and if desired in appropriate situations, offer the services of Christian workers for meeting the unfinished evangelistic task in the Pacific, e.g. in the field of youth work, etc.;

4. put on the conscience and sense of mission of the churches in the Pacific the whole matter of pastoral care and evangelism

among Asians living in the Pacific. We realize that in Fiji
there are over 200,000 Indians, over 6,000 Chinese in Tahiti,
and about 5,000 Javanese in New Caledonia ;

5. in the light of the experience we have had at this Conference,
we feel there is great gain to be achieved both for churches in
E. Asia and in the Pacific if a goodwill, evangelistic team from
the Pacific could visit some congregations in selected countries
in the E.A.C.C. area. We are willing to follow up this idea
in detail if the proposal proves acceptable and practicable.

APPENDIX 'B'

The Melanesian Brotherhood

Perhaps the most important thing about the Melanesian Brotherhood is that it is an indigenous growth.

In the year 1924, the Founder, Ini Kopuria, a sergeant of police,
whilst sick in hospital, received by a vision or dream a clear direction
from God that he should initiate that work which the Brothers have
ever since continued to do. He requested and received the Bishop's
approval for the formation of such a Brotherhood. He then toured
the Church Schools, explaining his ideas, and gained eight recruits.

From that simple start, the Brotherhood has grown, taking the
Gospel to many heathen parts of the Solomon Islands, the New
Hebrides, New Britain and New Guinea. Every year in October, all
Brothers except those on New Guinea service (who do a 3-year
period) gather together at the Mother House on Guadalcanal for
Retreat, Conference, new professions and new postings. Now 37
years old, the Brotherhood has nearly 100 members. The first two
Papuan Brothers took their Vows this year, and they hope to return
after experience in the Solomons to start a Papuan branch of the
work.

The Brothers live under what are generally known as the Three
"Religious" Vows, viz. Poverty, Chastity, Obedience.

1. Poverty. The Brothers receive no payment whatsoever, and
live a life which—even for Melanesians—is one of the utmost
simplicity.
2. Chastity. The Brothers remain unmarried, in order to serve
God in complete singleness of heart.
3. Obedience. The Brothers promise unquestioning obedience
to the Bishop as Father of all the Brothers, to the Head
Brother and to the Elder Brother of the particular Household
to which they are appointed.

Till recently, the Brothers used to take these Vows for a period of
one year at a time, being free at the conclusion of that period either
to leave the Brotherhood or to renew their Vows. At present, Vows
are taken for periods of 3 years at a time, after at least a year's
Noviciate. The present Head Brother, after 11 years as a Brother,
has this year gone to a "Religious" House in Australia to prepare for
his LIFE Vows. It is hoped that more will feel thus called.

A Brother, on Profession of Vows, is appointed to a Household. A Household consists of at least eight Brothers, who live communally. They are sent out only to entirely heathen areas, where they live a two-fold life:

1. A life of the daily round of adoration, private prayer and meditation, and a particular form of corporate prayer, morning and evening, known as the Brotherhood "Office", which always includes intercession for the heathen.

2. A life of service, whereby they identify themselves with the people amongst whom they live, winning their confidence by learning their language, helping them in their ordinary daily life and work, in their gardens and in their villages, visiting and praying with the sick, exorcizing devils, serving the widows, the aged and infirm, caring for orphans.

All this exhibition of Christian living and behaviour is prior to any particular preaching of Christian doctrine. Two by two, the Brothers visit villages for periods not exceeding a month before returning to derive from the common life of the Household renewed strength to go out again.

The Brothers endeavour to select in any given village one or more young men whom they take to live with them. They teach these men enough to be able to conduct village prayers and give simple instructions, and to be ready assistants for the teacher whom the Bishop will send to replace the Brothers when they move on.

There is no doubt that it is the depth of dedication and the joyful abandonment to the Brotherhood Life of communal prayer and service, under Vows and Rule, which largely give such spontaneity and punch to the Brothers' evangelistic work.

A further great source of strength to the Brothers' life and work are the groups of Companions, organized in very many villages to pray daily for the Brothers and for the conversion of the heathen and to support the work by their offerings.

Bp. David Hand
Leonard Alafurai

APPENDIX 'C'

Building Up the Congregation in Dutch New Guinea

Purpose: To renew and to deepen the spiritual life of the congregations and to inspire the ministers, pastors, elders and deacons for their work.

Means: Production of a monthly church paper; the publishing of study material in order to improve the preaching and teaching; promoting Bible study; deepening the insight into the task of the elders and deacons, and the function of the Sessions.

To initiate this movement there will be two conferences, each for a part of the Church. To these conferences will come *all* the ordained ministers.

Topics: Methods and practice of Bible study.
Method of teaching Bible and confirmation classes.
Instruction concerning the use of the booklet for Elders and
Deacons (dealing e.g. with pastoral care).
Discussion concerning the question: "Why am I a minister?"
The ministers are to bring these themes to the presbyteries, so that
the pastors and elders may be prepared to bring them before the
local congregation.

Ecumenical Team:

A new missionary enterprise has been started in the Highlands of
Dutch New Guinea by an ecumenical team. The work is done in
the Evangelical Christian Church. The composition of the team is:
A minister and two evangelists (trained) of the Evangelical
Christian Church.
Two missionaries from the Rhenish Mission (Barmen, Germany).
A medical doctor from the Dutch Reformed Church ("Oegst-
geest").

J. P. Kabel

Report of Commission C: The Relevance of the Gospel to Changing Conditions of Life

The first task of the Church in making plain the relevance of the
Gospel to changing conditions is to be faithful in its own life, in its
worship and fellowship, and in its proclamation of the Gospel, so
that the new humanity in Christ (Ephesians 2:15) may be manifest.
1. The Church must also relate its work to the changing conditions
of to-day. There are population movements from village to town in
many island groups; for example, in the Port Moresby area, New
Guinea, in 18 months the floating population increased from 500 to
1,500 people. In this situation the Churches must emphasise the
need for the pastoral care of their people in towns as well as in
villages. To help people to meet these new problems, sound training
must be given within families and Church. In order to help people
to meet the challenges of paid employment, new leisure periods, and
new conditions of personal relationship between employer and
employee, there must be sound basic training in the family and in
the Church in the early years. In particular, however, the churches
must develop their pastoral ministry and encourage members of congregations to participate in visitation to ensure the fullest possible
pastoral care. In some newly formed communities and in towns,
congregations have been formed on the initiative of the newcomers
to the areas, e.g. Gizo, Solomon Islands. We welcome such action
and hope that such congregations of newcomers will be received as

an integral part of the local church. It may also be necessary for churches in or near the towns to provide community centres for people far from their homes so that there is less opportunity or necessity to roam the streets, drink or gamble.

2. In many parts of the Pacific area there is drift from the old communal culture to a wage-earning economy. For some, this results in uncertainty about the Christian use of money and the things it buys. The Churches must give teaching on these matters to avoid abuses, and we suggest that the following points are important:

We are thankful to God for all the gifts that help us to live healthy and useful lives, but we are in danger of trusting in material things alone as sufficient for life.

The most precious things in life cannot be bought with money, and we must teach and pray that our people may receive the riches of faith.

Further, we must learn to accept material goods, new techniques and greater prosperity, as gifts of which we are the stewards, with responsibility to God, to the community in which we live, and to those in other lands whose state of poverty must claim our active attention.

3. In our islands there is an increasing desire for education. It is often sought in order that children may be trained for better jobs, and that our peoples may not be left behind in the modern world. We believe that education is part of our Christian development and must be directed to the glory of God. Our education is a failure if it leads us to be proud, or if it does not fit us to take a proper part in the life of our community. Life should be presented as a whole. The education of young people to the completion of secondary schooling should be in their own environment. This will fit them to consider with maturer judgment the challenges to their own culture. It will also enable them to take their proper place more easily in the pattern of life as it develops in the islands. For the present, however, they may also have to spend some time in other lands for post-secondary training.

4. The people of the Pacific are already becoming aware of the responsibilities which are or may soon be theirs in political affairs. It may be suggested to those who are gifted in ways which may serve the community well in politics, that they regard this as a genuine vocation, and that churches should support those who enter this field of responsibility by understanding, by prayer, and by sincere study of political problems. It should be remembered also that the pastors of our churches are going to be called upon for advice and information regarding these new developments, and they may profitably receive some help to this end in their training courses.

Bible References: Para. 1—Luke 15:3-7
Para. 2—Luke 12:15; Matthew 25:14-30
Para. 3—Romans 12:2
Para. 4—Romans 13:3-8

RESOLUTIONS

1. (a) That this Conference records its appreciation of the South Pacific Commission for its research programmes and other work which have been of great benefit to the islands.

(b) That this Conference records its conviction that increased educational opportunities should be available to children in the islands, and its appreciation to those Governments which are taking steps to this end.

(c) That this Conference records its conviction that higher education should be available within our island environment, and therefore urges the Governments in the Pacific, through the South Pacific Commission, to consider the establishment of a South Pacific University.

2. (*The following resolution, arising from a point raised in the Commission's discussion, was prepared by the Steering Committee of the Conference, and discussed and adopted by its Plenary Session*):
In view of the fact that nuclear tests have been held in the Pacific, the Conference expresses its gratitude for the continuing efforts of the World Council of Churches and the Commission of the Churches on International Affairs to secure the cessation of nuclear tests. The Conference urges the Churches in the Pacific area to pray for a successful outcome of the present Geneva Conference on the cessation of nuclear tests.

3. (*The following resolution, arising from a proposal brought to the Conference by the delegates from the Church in Tahiti, was considered by the Steering Committee of the Conference and amended and adopted by its Plenary Session. It is recorded under the Report of Commission C because of its relevance to the subject of that Commission's work. The French text below is that presented to the Conference. The English text embodies the revisions made by the Conference and is the resolution adopted by the Conference.*):
Demande de l'Eglise de Tahiti à la Conférence—L'Eglise Tahitienne, et toute la population de Polynésie orientale, se trouvent aujourd'hui devant de grands dangers, à cause de la main-mise croissante du Tourisme sur les Iles tahitiennes. Il est nécessaire d'apporter à l'Eglise des informations, des conseils, et de l'aide, dans l'intérèt du peuple tout entier.

Ayant pris connaissance de cette situation, la Conférence suggère qu'un spécialiste de ces problèmes, de préférence un Américain (la plupart des touristes étant américains) vienne, au nom du Conseil International des Missions, faire à Tahiti une enquète approfondie.

Resolution of the Conference
The Church in Tahiti, and all the population of eastern Polynesia as well, is now confronted by great dangers, because of the

increasing hold of the Tourist Industry over the Tahitian Islands. In the interests of the whole Tahitian nation, it is necessary to bring to the Church the information, the advice, and the help which she desperately needs.

In view of this situation, the Conference RESOLVES that a thorough enquiry be made, on behalf of the I.M.C., by some specialist, possibly an American (most of the tourists coming from the U.S.A.) into this and similar situations in the Pacific area.

Report of Commission D: The Place of Young People in the Life of the Church

Introduction—The New Testament provides abundant evidence of Christ's concern for children and young people.

In the terms of reference given to the Commission, young people are persons between the ages of twelve and twenty-five years.

I. YOUTH IN PACIFIC POPULATIONS

The Commission considered:

1. The large percentage of young people and children in Pacific populations—generally 45% under 15 years (54% under 18 years in West Solomon Islands; 62% under 21 years for Maoris in New Zealand).
2. The increasing opportunities for youth in the communities
   —the increasing number who are receiving secondary or higher education, including education abroad;
   —the increasing number of positions for employment available for young people. These often involve a person leaving home.

II. AIMS OF YOUNG PEOPLE'S WORK

These may be stated briefly as being "to prepare young people for life in the world as members of the household of faith".

A fuller statement would include:

1. to seek the commitment of young people to Jesus Christ, to prepare them for the world by developing spiritual life and to lead them to be effective Christian witnesses.
2. to assist in building the Church as a family in which young people have their rightful place.
3. to show the relevance of the gospel to the problems of young people, e.g. in relation to the opposite sex, preparation for marriage, the Church, political issues, etc.
4. to train for leadership in both Church and community.
5. to provide constructive recreational and training activities, and instruction in the right use of leisure.
6. to encourage young people to take part in service in home, Church and community.

III. SOME ISSUES FOR YOUNG PEOPLE

Young people need the guidance they will receive as a result of informed discussion in the fellowship of the Church on the position of the Christian in issues arising from:

1. *Political and social change.*
National independence movements. In some places there is much discussion, in other places a reluctance to discuss the issues arising. Political matters, including such matters as forms of local and central government, trade unions, strikes, land tenure.

Movement from villages to larger centres, involving break-up of family and tribal customs, poor housing conditions, economic differences and poverty, delinquency, liquor problems, attitude to money.

2. *Inadequacy of education, especially an understanding of the Bible.* Difficulties are arising in interpreting the meaning of scientific advances. For example, in some areas the view is taken that the development of satellites is an act of pride and interference with God's realm. The interpretation of the creation narratives in Genesis in relation to scientific developments poses problems for some. Some ministers and pastors are not equipped to answer queries on the Bible and contemporary problems. The interpretation of natural phenomena also raises difficulties, e.g. how the recent hurricane in Tonga is to be understood in relation to God's purpose of love.

3. *Marriage.* The questions on which guidance is needed include the refusal of parents to allow personal choice of partner in marriage, the effects of the rise in the amount required for the "bride price" and in the cost of exchange of gifts and marriage feast, polygamy, divorce and unions outside the marriage bond, premarital inchastity.

IV. A SURVEY OF YOUTH WORK

Some principles were discovered which should guide all youth work:

1. Any programme or activity should be relevant to the age or stage for which it is designed, e.g. graded lessons in Sunday schools, youth groups working within clearly defined age limits.

2. The local church youth programme needs the stimulus of the wider conference and camp activities. In this regard, an extension of inter-church activities would be of great benefit.

3. Every effort should be made to avoid overlapping or competition between different youth organizations and programmes.

The list below provides a basis for further thought and planning:

(a) *Local*, i.e. in a village or town: Family church—upper part of Sunday School—Bible class—Boys' Brigade—Girls' Life Brigade —Boy Scouts—Girl Guides—mixed youth clubs—hobby clubs, e.g. woodwork club—sporting clubs—teacher and/or leader training.

(b) *District*, i.e. in a group of churches or villages: Youth rallies— Bible school—youth camps.

(c) *Headquarters*: Appointment of part-time or full-time secretary or youth trainer—youth camps—Youth Leaders' Training School —youth training for Ministry—topics in the Church magazine—a small paper.

(d) *Some special aids and activities*: Visual aids—films and film-strips—literature and pamphlets—"Pacific Island World"—work camps—"Melanesian Brotherhood" (see appendix B to Report of Commission B)—"Torchbearer" organization in Papua, an organization for boys and girls in the age group 14-18, which appoints its own officers and is responsible for its own activities, the pastor working with it in an advisory capacity and a deacon being chairman. Its activities in the weekly meeting include prayer, Bible study and visitation.

RESOLUTIONS

1. That our churches be urged to consider courageously the issues facing their young people and to assist them in meeting them.

2. That our churches be urged to meet with their young people in the hope of finding together ways in which young people can take an active share in the mission of the whole Church fellowship.

Report of Commission E: The Christian Family

1. It has only been possible for this Commission to open up this complex subject of the Christian Family, and to deal in particular with its foundation in Christian marriage. It was made abundantly clear that there is need for the churches in the different areas to study the subject in greater depth and detail.

The Commission found that marriage patterns and family systems differ considerably from territory to territory, which rendered the problem more complex. Bride prices, arranged marriages and the growing desire of young people to marry according to their own choice are some examples of the various problems.

The Commission also found that the various areas are at different stages of development and so the Church's approach to marriage and marriage problems must necessarily vary. For example, in most parts of Papua and New Guinea and in other places, marriages according to local custom are very common, or may be said to be the order of the day. In other more developed areas, a more or less set pattern is followed.

Whilst it is perhaps regrettable to disturb this social pattern of life, we as Christians should nevertheless define clearly our Christian ideal of marriage, and above all instruct our people accordingly, aiming at the bringing about of self-control, both for the parents and young people.

We consider therefore that there is a need for a statement by the churches, re-emphasising the Christian teaching regarding marriage.

2. The Purpose of Marriage is:
  (a) sharing in the creative activity of God by procreation;
  (b) fulfilment of the personality and happiness of man and woman according to God's Law;
  (c) rearing of children to the glory of God;
  (d) for the welfare and stability of human society.

A Christian Doctrine of Marriage is based on the Bible, expressed in the form and order of marriage services, and confirmed by Christian thinking and experience.

3. The Commission urges that the Church accept the responsibility of helping its members and the community to a Christian view of sex and marriage, and suggests that the Church provide training and facilities for:
  (a) sex education of children and adolescents;
  (b) marriage guidance for young people in preparation for marriage;
  (c) marriage counselling for married people and family counselling for parents who require help in Christian family life.

Literature is needed for this purpose. This must be closely related to the cultural background and the immediate problems of the society concerned. This literature needs to be at two levels, written and published:
  (i) for the training of pastors and leaders;
  (ii) for adolescents, young marrieds and parents.

A thorough course in the Christian Doctrine of Marriage should be given in every theological college. The Commission feels that, next to parents, pastors often have the most contact with young people. Therefore, every pastor should receive training in how to advise young people with respect to marriage. Missionaries from outside the area, who are engaged in such training, should first make a thorough study of the cultural background of the people. Appropriate literature should be placed in the hands of these pastors that they may more thoroughly and effectively do their work.

4. The Marriage Ceremonies should be more meaningful. It was felt that there were and still are customs in the indigenous social orders which could be adapted to a Christian marriage ceremony, such as the bridal couple eating together, e.g. a sweet potato or some other food, the placing of a large bamboo ring over the couple by the elders to signify that they are one. The Western marriage ceremony, as it is performed in many missions, is not fully understood by the islanders, and therefore cannot appeal to them. Christian marriage services, with symbolism and ritual meaningful to the people of the area concerned, should be worked out wherever possible.

5. Various customs in which older members of the two families concerned arrange marriages for young men and young women, with little or no regard to the wishes of the young people, were discussed. It was found that such "arranged marriages" have thus far proved more stable than marriages planned only by the two young people

themselves. In those areas where the payment of a "bride price" is a part of the marriage pattern, the increasing awareness of the value of money is causing an inflation of the bride price. Since this causes hardship for many poor young men, attempts are being made to abolish or control this custom in some areas.

It was noted that in some ways the larger "extended family" seems to be favourable to Christian development, whereas in the smaller "nuclear family" tensions often arise to make such development difficult.

In areas under French rule, where the law requires a civil ceremony in addition to and prior to any church ceremony, the matter of the civil registration of marriages is more important than in some other areas. The church relation to civil registration needs to be examined in some areas, e.g. parts of Papua / New Guinea.

It was also noted that divorces seem to be increasing in many areas, but we did not have time to discuss this problem thoroughly, nor the more recently proposed matter of "Family Planning".

RESOLUTIONS

1. That this Conference draws the urgent attention of the churches to the issues raised in the above report.

2. That this Conference requests its Continuation Committee to give early attention to these issues.

General Resolutions of the Conference

I. ON CHURCH RELATIONSHIPS IN THE PACIFIC

This Conference has experienced the value of the meeting together of representatives of churches and missions from different areas and different church traditions. It has also heard the views of many of its Island members on the need for closer relations between the churches in the Pacific. Having considered these things, the Conference sends the following message to the churches represented at it.

This first Conference of Churches and Missions in the Pacific strongly desires that the churches in the South Pacific should speedily learn to know one another more fully, to work together more closely and to trust one another more readily. It recognizes that this will call for a new attitude of mind within the churches, and a willingness to meet and work with other churches without mistrust. It is considered that this is necessary if the responsibility we share together to proclaim one Lord is to be rightly discharged.

It therefore recommends to the churches that they give earnest attention to the reports of the Commissions and related resolutions, and to the following suggestions, and act upon those which are possible in each area.

1. *Ways in which neighbouring churches may get to know each other* (both within one island group and in neighbouring island groups):
   (a) Invite fraternal delegates from other churches to church assemblies or similar bodies.
   (b) Invite pastors to share in the life of a neighbouring church for a few months.
   (c) Invite youth delegates from other churches to share in youth activities (e.g. youth camps) (see also report of Commission D).
   (d) Arrange occasional meetings of youth leaders of different churches to discuss their work together.
   (e) Arrange occasional meetings of the leaders of women's groups of different churches to discuss their work together, and with a view to increased co-operation of men and women in church and society.

2. *Ways in which neighbouring churches may work together.*
   (a) In youth organizations, including where appropriate, the Student Christian Movement (see also report of Commission D).
   (b) In providing secondary education.
   (c) The staffs of theological colleges may help in each other's colleges. (Note: A separate resolution about a united theological college for the South Pacific will be found under the report of Commission A.)
   (d) By providing together Christian radio programmes (see also report of Commission B).
   (e) In some areas a local Christian council may be formed through which the churches may think and act together.
   (f) By joint evangelistic activities, especially in growing centres of population (see reports of Commissions B and C).

II. ON ARRANGEMENTS FOR CONTINUING THE WORK OF THE CONFERENCE

1. *Continuation Committee.* The Conference realizes that it has only begun the study of the subjects it has considered, and has only begun the task of helping the churches and missions to know each other and help each other throughout the Pacific area. If what has been achieved through this Conference is not to be lost, some arrangements are necessary to carry it on. These must be based primarily in the area of the Conference. The Conference therefore RESOLVES—
   (a) To set up a Continuation Committee to carry forward the studies and discussions begun at this Conference, and to consult with the churches regarding the development of co-operation among them.

(b) To ask each member of the Continuation Committee to take the main responsibility for one of the subjects discussed at this Conference.

(c) To authorise the Committee to act for a period not exceeding five years. In good time before the expiry of this period, the Committee is instructed to consult with the churches represented in this Conference, and with the World Council of Churches, regarding continuing arrangements for its work.

(d) To appoint the following as members of the Continuation Committee, subject to the approval of the churches to which they severally belong. In the event of any member being unable to act, the church to which he belongs is entitled to nominate a substitute to the Committee for appointment in his place. The following initial allocation of responsibilities is suggested to the Committee:

Chairman
    Rev. S. A. Tuilovoni   (M)   Fiji
A. Ministry
    Rev. A. G. Horwell   (P)   New Hebrides
B. Unfinished Task
    Rev. L. Alafurai   (A)   Solomon Islands
C. Changing Conditions
    Rev. M. A. Ledoux   (E.Ch)   New Caledonia
D. Young People
    Mr. Stahl Mileng   (L)   New Guinea
E. Christian Family
    Mrs. Fetaui Mataafa   (C)   Samoa

(e) The Continuation Committee is instructed to consult the churches regularly regarding its work. It is not authorised to make public pronouncements.

(f) The persons named above are requested to meet as a provisional Continuation Committee at the close of this Conference.

2. *Secretary.* The Conference thus recognizes that the main responsibility for carrying the work of the Conference further rests in the churches who have been represented at it. At the same time it realizes that our churches will need help in doing this, especially in the early stages. It therefore RESOLVES—

To request the International Missionary Council to consider the possibility of giving such help, by providing financial assistance to the Continuation Committee to help it to meet from time to time. It further requests the International Missionary Council, if possible, to appoint a secretary, on the nomination of the Continuation Committee and responsible to it, and provide funds for travel and office expenses. This secretary would live in the area and travel throughout it and so be a living link between the churches and assist the Committee in carrying further the work begun at this Conference.

3. *Report of the Conference.* The Conference RESOLVES—
That the officers of the Conference be authorized to edit and publish the records of the Conference.

III. APPRECIATION

The Conference RESOLVES—

THAT this Conference of Churches and Missions in the Pacific records its deep gratitude to the Samoan Church (L.M.S.) and the Methodist Church in Samoa for inviting the Conference to meet in Samoa, for the most generous and gracious hospitality extended to it by the churches and their organizations and members, and for all the thought and care for the well-being of the Conference and its work given by the Local Arrangements Committee and the Staff and students of Malua College. This overflowing service has not only made the Conference possible but has given its members such a memorably happy stay in Samoa, and they are profoundly grateful;

THAT the delegates to the Conference wish to assure the people of Western Samoa, through their Council of State, of our appreciation of the gracious welcome everywhere extended to us during the period of our stay in Western Samoa, and of our prayers for God's blessing on the outcome of the forthcoming plebiscite and on the future of the Samoan people;

THAT the Conference expresses its thanks to the Methodist Church in Fiji for making the services of Miss Allison M. Down available to assist in the preparation of the Conference and to serve as its secretary during its meeting; and to Miss Down for her invaluable assistance in preparing for the Conference, especially in handling travel arrangements, and for her ready help in every way during the Conference;

THAT the Conference expresses its gratitude to all the members who have contributed in such a variety of ways to its life and work. The Conference has been a truly co-operative effort, every member contributing his share to its work in one capacity or another. For this willingness on the part of each to contribute to the whole, the Conference is grateful;

THAT the members of the Conference gives thanks to God that He led the International Missionary Council to call this Conference and so actually to bring us together. We would like to record our appreciation of the great amount of work that the I.M.C. secretaries have put into the organization of this Conference, and especially of the contribution that the Rev. R. K. Orchard has made in seeing that consideration of great issues and a multitude of details have together contributed to the unity that we have found in this our first meeting together.

Sermon preached at the
Concluding Service of Worship

by Bishop Lesslie Newbigin

Our first thought at the end of this Conference is surely one of thankfulness. It has been good for us to be here—surrounded by the loving care of our hosts, upheld by the prayers of those who sent us, encouraged by the mutual sharing of our varied experiences, and above all nourished afresh by the Word of God. Surely we all want to thank God for His goodness, and that is the first purpose of this service.

But surely also this Conference has disturbed us. We have seen, perhaps more vividly than before, how the winds of change that are blowing so insistently all over the world, are blowing into the Pacific too, disturbing and uprooting many things that had stood secure for centuries. We have perhaps been disturbed by new ideas, by things which compelled us to re-think long-held convictions. And above all we have surely been disturbed as we have studied the Word of God together. We have seen many things in a new light, and perhaps we have been compelled to see that things in our own lives and the lives of our churches are evidences of bondage rather than freedom, of the law rather than the Gospel. Surely there is not one of us who has not been disturbed, compelled to look at many things in new ways, compelled to question what we had taken for granted.

Now we are to go back home. If we know ourselves at all, we know how easy it will be to slip back into exactly the place where we were before we set out. There will be a pile of arrears of work to cope with. There will be the old problems, the old tasks, the old assumptions and expectations surrounding us. What shall we do? Shall we make a terrific effort to shift things just a little bit in the direction we have seen, before we are forced back again into the old rut? I remember a group of students at a conference who were taking themselves terribly seriously. That great Methodist saint, W. R. Maltby was listening to their discussions. After some time he chipped in and said: "I would advise you first of all to banish the word 'try' altogether from your vocabulary. The Christian life isn't first a matter of trying; it's a matter of receiving a gift". They listened earnestly, and then one of them said: "All right, Dr. Maltby, we will try to remember".

We do not go back first of all to try. We go back, I hope, with a new sense of what God has done, is doing, and will do. We have thought much of Abraham in this Conference, and so I have chosen as my text this verse:

> "By faith, Abraham when he was called to go out into a place which he should after receive for an inheritance, obeyed; and he went out, not knowing whither he went" (Hebrews 11:8).

God, who called Abraham, has called us. The story of salvation did not begin with a decision of Abraham, but with a decision of God.

God called Abraham and he obeyed. He has called us. He brought us here. It is He who gave us that discontent with what we are and what our churches are which we have known here. It is a sign of His grace which goes before all our decisions. If He has in any degree made us strangers and pilgrims, as Abraham was; if He has in any sense said: "Get up and get out to the place I will show you", that is His grace. He has already taken action. And He does not mock us or play around with our lives, though it is sometimes terribly hard to know where He is leading us. Our first business is simply to heed that call, trust and obey.

I think we shall all of us carry away from this Conference Hans-Ruedi Weber's pictures of the history of salvation, with the pilgrim Abraham as the pioneer striding forth with his staff in his hand, and the pilgrim people hand in hand, marching from the Cross to the Holy City. There were two things in that second picture which made it different from the picture of Abraham the solitary nomad. Firstly, that there was a company of people holding hands, supporting each other. Secondly, that there was above their heads the heavenly dove—the living Spirit of God.

We are that people. We are like Abraham—we do not know where we are going; but we know who has called us and who is leading us. We do not know where we are going. We have no blue-print of the future. God has not given it. But we know who has called us, and who is leading us. I want to stress this point. The Bible tells us over and over again that we are called to be pilgrims, to live in tents, to be ever moving on. This whole chapter is a sort of roll-call of the pilgrim people who

"all died in faith, not having received the promises, but having seen them afar off, and were persuaded of them, and embraced them, and confessed that they were strangers and pilgrims on the earth. They then that say such things declare plainly that they seek a country. And truly, if they had been mindful of that country from whence they came out, they might have had opportunity to have returned. But now they desire a better country, that is, an heavenly: wherefore God is not ashamed to be called their God: for He hath prepared for them a city".

God's people is a pilgrim people, not desiring to settle down anywhere short of the Holy City.

But we do not just wander about. We have a guide. And we can trust Him. It is terribly important to insist on this. The Holy Spirit is able to guide us. I want to give a small piece of personal testimony here. You know that in most of our church work we work with rules and customs which settle a vast number of questions for us in advance. Of course, much of this is necessary, but it can easily happen that these rules come between us and the experience of daily dependence on the Spirit. During the past 13 years I lived in a Church which had inherited a great many different customs from Anglican, Presbyterian, Methodist, L.M.S. and other traditions.

You can carry on church life fairly easily with one book of rules ; but if you have four books of rules, all infallible and all contradicting each other, then you are in a difficulty. You are simply forced to go behind the books of rules to the Holy Scriptures, and ask what the Spirit has to tell you. That was what happened to us in South India. Over and over again we found that we were simply forced to go behind the traditional rules and sit down with the Bible and ask : "What does the Holy Spirit teach us from Scripture about our duty now in India in 1961?". This has led to some startling new discoveries for all of us ; but it has also given us a very deep assurance that the Spirit really can guide.

I think we have had some experience of this in our Bible studies here. We know that there are great differences among us. At this Conference we have hardly begun to face them. We have not really come to the point where we could face our deepest differences frankly and learn from one another ; such differences, for instance, as those which make it difficult for us to join together at the Lord's Table. We should not be too much discouraged by them. If we are faithful, the time for the real facing of these differences will come. But we do know, and this Conference has surely deepened this knowledge, that there is one place where we all meet to receive renewal and re-direction. It is the place where we sit down together with the Bible, asking God the Holy Spirit to take the things of Christ which are testified in Scripture and show them to us afresh.

I hope that when we go from here we shall not let this experience be forgotten. We read the Bible much ; we quote it ; we use it to prove our points ; but how much do we let it speak to us—or rather let the Holy Spirit speak to us through its words? How much do we—usually—really *listen*? I think perhaps some of the most fruitful moments of this Conference have been the moments when we sat together with the text of scripture and tried to write down exactly what the text said about certain questions. We had to struggle to get away from our usual habit of writing down what we already thought, and really to listen to what the text said. Is it not tremendously important that we continue to do what we have been doing here, training ourselves together to listen to what the Spirit says to us through the Word as we face the new situations of each day?

If we learn to do this, we shall not be afraid of change and disturbance. It is human to fear change. It is natural that the pilgrim people should sometimes want to dig itself in and establish some sort of permanent settlement where things are at least a fair attempt to look like the Holy City. But God drives us out of these settlements of ours. It may sometimes be very painful, but it is necessary. Things cannot remain as they are, because God has better things in store for us, things which can only be won by those ready to take risks and face dangers. This call to become a stranger and pilgrim comes to the Church again and again. When it comes, we must accept it as a sign of God's grace, a sign that He has not forgotten

His Church or given it over to the enemy. If we go back from this Conference disturbed, and aware of greater disturbances to come, that is to be accepted with a thankful obedience to the calling of God, and a trustful acceptance of the daily guidance of the Holy Spirit.

But in all this we are to be a pilgrim *people,* not a set of solitary nomads. The figures in the second picture were joining hands. It is surely of God's mercy that He has given us here at Malua a glimpse of the fellow-pilgrims with whom we share this calling. This whole meeting is surely just a tightening of the brotherly grip on each other's hands. We must not let that grip grow slack. One word that went to the hearts of all who heard it was surely Pastor Kenape's word in his sermon here on Sunday: "I never prayed for the Church in New Caledonia". Can we not resolve here that we will take the Conference list of delegates and incorporate it in our regular schemes of private intercession, so that we shall all be continuing to uphold one another in prayer? That is surely a very big part of the meaning of that hand-grip in the picture. It is too easy just to say in general that we shall pray for one another. Real prayer takes time and thought. Let us not leave here without determining that we shall take the time and thought needed to uphold one another in persistent and intelligent and believing prayer.

Very specially must we pray for the members of the Continuation Committee which we have appointed, for its Chairman, and for the Secretary whom we hope—if God wills—to appoint. Their work over the coming years can surely help us to be more truly one pilgrim people—one marching band, and not a series of scattered and isolated wanderers. And if, in course of time, ways appear in which we can do certain things together for God's glory, we shall surely welcome them and put our best efforts into them.

We do not know where we are going, but we know who has called us and who is guiding us. And we know one thing more; we know that God has promised us an inheritance. He has prepared for His pilgrim people a city. We *know.* Deeply and finally, we know— through Jesus Christ—that all will be well in the end; that however long the journey, journeys will end in lovers' meeting—because He, the great Lover, is coming to meet us. As Luther said: "He has given us all, forgiven us all, and promised us all; so that we lack only faith to believe it". What we need is not so much to try harder as to believe more simply. *He* called us—that is why we are strangers and pilgrims, why we are on the move, why we can never be content. He called us to go out. He is with us to guide us. He is at the end to receive us as heirs of His everlasting joy.

Believe that, and all else follows.

Who's Who

ALAFURAI, REV. LEONARD.   Rural Dean of Malaita.   Formerly teacher, Pawa.
Address: Melanesian Mission, Auki, Malaita, British Solomon Islands.   Anglican
ALI, MR. SULTAN.   Headmaster, Methodist Mission School, Ba ; member, Indian Government-appointed Advisory Committee, Ba ; local preacher ; senior Circuit Steward, Ba/Ra.   Formerly Chairman, Ba branch of Fiji Teachers' Union ; Headmaster of Vatulaulau Indian Committee School.
Address: Namosau Methodist School, Ba, Fiji.   Methodist
ANDREWS, REV. STANLEY GEORGE.   General Secretary, Overseas Missions Department, Methodist Church of New Zealand.   Formerly missionary in Fiji ; Principal, Davuilevu Educational Centre.
Address: Box 5023, Auckland, C.1, New Zealand.
                                              (*Observer*) Methodist
BALOILOI, MR. ENOSI.   Pastor-teacher.   Formerly Government scholar at Sogeri Training Institute, Papua.   Held John Dixon Scholarship for Youth Leadership training, Australia.
Address: Methodist Church, Salamo, via Samarai, Papua.
                                                         Methodist
BARNES, REV. ROLAND L.   Chairman, Papua New Guinea District of Methodist Church.   Formerly missionary in New Britain and Papua.
Address: Methodist Mission, Tari, via Goroka, T.P.N.G.
                                                         Methodist
BEVILACQUA, REV. JOSEPH J.   Associate General Secretary, Hawaiian Evangelical Association.   Formerly Director of work in Puerto Rico ; service in U.S.A.
Address: 2103 Nuuanu Avenue, Honolulu 17, Hawaii.
                                   (*Consultant*) Congregational
BOGOTU, MR. FRANCIS.   Asst. master, Pawa Mission School.
Address: Melanesian Mission, Marovovo, British Solomon Islands.
                                                         Anglican
BRADSHAW, REV. DR. JOHN.   Principal, Malua Theological College.
Address: Malua Theological College, Malua, W. Samoa.
                                                  Congregational
CHIU, REV. BAN IT.   Home Secretary, Australian Board of Missions.   Formerly Vicar of Selangor ; member, Interim Committee E.A.C.C.
Address: 14 Spring Street, Sydney, New South Wales, Australia.
                                            (*Observer*) Anglican
COCKS, REV. NORMAN H. F.   Secretary in Australia and New Zealand, London Missionary Society (with administrative responsibility for work of L.M.S. in Papua and Nauru).
Address: 41 The Boulevarde, Petersham, New South Wales, Australia.   (*Observer*) Congregational
COWLED, REV. STANLEY G. C., O.B.E.   Chairman, Fiji-Fijian District and United District of Methodist Church in Fiji.   Formerly missionary

to Papua ; Senior Chaplain, Fiji Military Forces ; member, Legislative Council, Fiji.

Address: P. O. Box 357, Suva, Fiji.   Methodist

CRAIG, REV. CHARLES STUART. Secretary for India, East Asia and Islands, London Missionary Society. Formerly missionary, China ; member of staff, S.C.M.

Address: 11 Carteret Street, London, S.W.1.

(*Observer*) Congregational

DOWN, MISS ALLISON M. Secretary, Methodist Church Office, Suva, Fiji.

Address: P.O. Box 357, Suva, Fiji.   (*Staff*) Methodist

DUNCAN, REV. DONALD E. Assistant Secretary, Overseas Missions Committee, Presbyterian Church of New Zealand. Formerly member, Maori Missions Committee ; Convener, Joint Maori Synod and General Assembly Committee.

Address: P.O. Box 110, Auckland, C.1, New Zealand.

(*Observer*) Presbyterian

EHU, DEACON TETUANUI. Deacon of the Isles under the Wind.

Address: c/o Conseil Superieur des Eglises Tahitiennes, Papeete, Tahiti.   Presbyterian

FORMAN, REV. DR. CHARLES W. Professor, Yale University Divinity School. Formerly Associate Director, Theological Education Fund of the International Missionary Council.

Address: c/o T.E.F., 475 Riverside Drive, New York, 27, U.S.A.

(*Consultant*) Presbyterian

FRERICHS, REV. DR. ALBERT C. V/President, Lutheran Mission New Guinea ; Headmaster, Heldsbach Area School.

Address: Lutheran Mission, Finschhafen, Territory of New Guinea.

Lutheran

FULLERTON, REV. L. DOUGLAS. Chairman, Fiji-Indian District of Methodist Church.

Address: P.O. Box 357, Suva, Fiji.   Methodist

GAIUS, REV. SAIMON. Minister on Probation. Attended Youth Conferences, Australia.

Address: Methodist Church, Rabaul, Territory of New Guinea.

Methodist

GRIBBLE, REV. CECIL F., O.B.E. General Secretary, Department of Overseas Missions, Methodist Church of Australasia. Formerly principal, Tupou Wesleyan College, Tonga ; Director of Education, Government of Tonga.

Address: 139 Castlereagh Street, Sydney, New South Wales.

(*Observer*) Methodist

GUISE, MR. JOHN.

Address: c/o Bishop of New Guinea, Dogura, via Samarai, T.P.N.G.   Anglican

HAND, RT. REV. GEOFFREY DAVID. Bishop Coadjutor, Diocese of New Guinea. Formerly missionary, New Guinea.

Address: Anglican Mission, Madang, New Guinea.   Anglican

HANLIN, REV. DR. HAROLD. Field Representative, Micronesia Mission of American Board of Commissioners for Foreign Missions ; work on translation and revision of Bible portions. Formerly Chaplain to U.S.A. Forces, Micronesia.
Address: American Board Mission, Ponape, E. Carolines.
Congregational

HAVEA, REV. DR. SIONE 'A. Head Tutor, Tupou College for Boys ; Secretary of Conference of Free Wesleyan Church of Tonga.
Address: Tupou College, Nuku'alofa, Tonga. Methodist

HEINE, REV. JOHN. Principal, Laura Intermediate School. Formerly on staff of Pastors-Teachers Training School.
Address: American Board Mission, Majuro Dist., Marshall Islands.
Congregational

HORWELL, REV. A. G. District missionary ; Clerk of the Assembly, Presbyterian Church of New Hebrides.
Address: Lamenu Island, via Vila, New Hebrides. Presbyterian

IOTAMA, REV. SEVE. Pastor of Niutao Church.
Address: Niutao Church, Niutao, Ellice Islands. Congregational

JONATHAN, PASTOR. Pastoral charge, Big Nambas territory.
Address: South West Bay, Malekula, New Hebrides. Presbyterian

JONES, REV. EMLYN. Chairman, Gilbert Islands District Committee ; Chairman, Church Administration Council ; Principal, Theological College.
Address: Tangintebu, Tarawa, Gilbert Islands. Congregational

KABEL, REV. JOHANNES P. Rector, Theological School. Formerly District missionary.
Address: Theologische School E.C.K., P.O. Box 115, Hollandia-Binnen, Dutch New Guinea. Presbyterian

KALAPU, MR. LUAFATASAGE. Speaker, Legislative Assembly of Government of W. Samoa ; Deacon and Lay Preacher, Samoan Church (L.M.S.).
Address: P.O. Box 331, Apia, W. Samoa. Congregational

KAUTAU, REV. AFELISI.
Address: P.O. Box 25, Makatugi, Alofi, Niue Island. Congregational

KEMPTHORNE, RT. REV. L. S. Bishop in Polynesia.
Address: Bishop's House, P.O. Box 35, Suva, Fiji. Anglican

KISIU, MR. MISIEL. Teacher, New Britain. Formerly pastor/teacher, New Guinea.
Address: Methodist Church, Vunairima, via Rabaul, New Guinea.
Methodist

LEDOUX, REV. MARC ANDRE. Delegate (Permanent Representative) of Société des Missions Evangeliques de Paris in New Caledonia. Formerly Youth Secretary, Madagascar ; Secretary for social problems, public relations and youth at Paris H.Q.
Address: B.P. 277, Noumea, New Caledonia.
(*Observer*) Presbyterian

LESSER, MOST REV. NORMAN A. Archbishop of New Zealand; Bishop of Waiapu. Formerly missionary to Kenya.
Address: Bishop's Court, Napier, New Zealand.   Anglican
MADDOX, REV. RUSSELL. Chairman, Samoan District of Methodist Church. Formerly member of Board of Missions, Methodist Church of Australasia.
Address: Methodist Church, Apia, W. Samoa.   Methodist
MADINE, REV. XOWIE. President, Evangelical Church of New Caledonia; Pastor, Island of Lifou.
Address: Chépénéhé, Lifou, New Caledonia.   Presbyterian
MAILEI, MR. TALA. Education Officer, Samoan Government. Formerly holder of travelling scholarships to New Zealand and U.S.A.
Address: Methodist Church, Apia, W. Samoa.   Methodist
MALOALI, REV. WILLEM. Teacher, Evangelist's School, Evangelical Christian Church of Dutch New Guinea.
Address: Sekolah Pengindjil, Ransiki, via Marokwar, Dutch New Guinea.   Presbyterian
MARINO, MR. JOSHUA. Asst. principal, Palau High School. Formerly Asst. Superintendent of Schools.
Address: Koror, Palau Islands, Caroline Islands.   Congregational
MATAAFA, MRS. FETAUI. Member of staff, Malifa School of Government of W. Samoa. Formerly teacher, Samoa College.
Address: P.O. Box 469, Apia, W. Samoa.   Congregational
MEA, PASTOR RETAU. Chairman, Papuan Church Assembly; pastor, Hanuabada.
Address: P.O. Box 83, Port Moresby, Papua.   Congregational
METAI, REV. KAITARA. Member, Church Administration Council; member of staff, Theological College. Formerly assisted in revision of Gilbertese Bible.
Address: Tangintebu, Tarawa, Gilbert Islands.   Congregational
MILENG, MR. STAHL. Asst. to Training Master, Teacher Training Centre, Madang.
Address: Lutheran Mission, Madang, New Guinea.   Lutheran
MO'UNGALOA, REV. VILIAMI H. Director of Youth Work, Free Wesleyan Church of Tonga. Formerly Senior Tutor, Sai'atoutai Bible School.
Address: P.O. Box 57, Nuku'alofa, Tonga.   Methodist
NABWAKULEA, MR. SETEPANO. Pastor/teacher, Mendi Circuit, Methodist Church of Papua.
Address: Methodist Mission, Tari, via Goroka, T.P.N.G.
            Methodist
NEWBIGIN, RT. REV. LESSLIE. General Secretary, International Missionary Council. Formerly Church of Scotland missionary to India; Bishop of Madurai, Church of South India; Chairman, I.M.C.
Address: Edinburgh House, 2 Eaton Gate, London, S.W.1.
            (*Consultant*) Church of South India

ORCHARD, REV. RONALD K. London Secretary, International Missionary Council. Formerly Foreign Secretary for Africa and East Asia, London Missionary Society.
Address: Edinburgh House, 2 Eaton Gate, London, S.W.1.
(Consultant) Congregational
OSBORNE, REV. KENNETH B. Missionary in charge of men's work, evangelism, agricultural development.
Address: Baptist Mission, Baiyer River, Free Mail Bag, Goroka, T.P.N.G. Baptist
PATH, REV. TITUS. Work among heathen tribes on Santo. Formerly lecturer, Tangoa Training Institute, Santo.
Address: Hog Harbour, Santo, New Hebrides. Presbyterian
PERE, REV. TA UPU. Youth and Education Secretary, Cook Islands Christian Church (L.M.S.).
Address: P.O. Box 93, Rarotonga, Cook Islands. Congregational
PERRY, REV. RAYMOND. Principal, Lawes College.
Address: Lawes College, Fife Bay, via Samarai, T.P.N.G.
Congregational
PIDJO, REV. TEIN W. Pastor in "strategic" centre of Koumac.
Address: B.P. 277, Noumea, New Caledonia. Presbyterian
PILOT, REV. BOGGO. Priest in charge, Badu Island.
Address: Church Office, Thursday Island, Queensland, Australia.
Anglican
PONS, REV. JACQUES. Teacher, Do-Neva Secondary School.
Address: Société des Missions Evangeliques de Paris, Do-Neva, Houailou, New Caledonia. *(Interpreter)* Presbyterian
RAAPOTO, REV. SAMUELA. General Secretary, Conseil Superieur des Eglises Tahitiennes.
Address: Conseil Superieur des Eglises Tahitiennes, Papeete, Tahiti.
Presbyterian
RAWCLIFFE, VEN. DEREK A. Archdeacon of Southern Melanesia. Formerly Asst. master, Pawa Senior School; Headmaster, Maravovo School.
Address: Melanesian Mission, Lolowai, Aoba, New Hebrides.
Anglican
ROBINSON, REV. WALTER W. Superintendent, Anglican Indian Mission, Labasa.
Address: P.O. Box 29, Labasa, Fiji. Anglican
SAPOLU, PASTOR-ELDER MILA. Vice-Chairman, Samoan Church (L.M.S.); Pastor, village of Solosolo.
Address: L.M.S. Solosolo, Apia, W. Samoa. Congregational
SEIDENBINDER, REV. PIERRE. Principal, Ecole Pastorale. Formerly Youth work, Gabon.
Address: Ecole Pastorale, Do-Neva, New Caledonia. Presbyterian
SOEJATNO, REV. ARDI.
Address: East Java Christian Church, Djalan Residen Sudikman 9, Surabaja, Java, Indonesia.
(Fraternal Representative E.A.C.C.) Reformed

STUCKEY, REV. JAMES M. General Secretary, Australian Presbyterian Board of Missions. Formerly missionary to Korea.
Address: Box 100, G.P.O. Sydney, New South Wales, Australia.
(*Observer*) Presbyterian
TAMAHORI, REV. JOHN T. Chaplain, Te Aute College, New Zealand. Formerly missionary to Tonga.
Address: c/o Bishop in Polynesia, P.O. Box 35, Suva, Fiji. Anglican
THAN, U KYAW. Associate General Secretary, East Asia Christian Conference. Formerly Assoc. General Secretary, W.S.C.F.; Tutor in History, University of Rangoon.
Address: 140 Pyi-daungsu-yeiktha Road, Rangoon, Burma.
(*Consultant*) Baptist
THOROGOOD, REV. BERNARD G. President of the Assembly, Cook Islands Christian Church ; Principal, Takoma College, Rarotonga.
Address: P.O. Box 93, Rarotonga, Cook Islands. Congregational
TUILOVONI, REV. SETAREKI A., M.B.E. Director, Methodist Young People's Department ; member, Standing Committee on the Ministry, I.M.C. Formerly teacher.
Address: P.O. Box 8, Nausori, Fiji. Methodist
VERNIER, REV. HENRI. President of Missions Evangéliques de Paris in Tahiti.
Address: Ecole Pastorale, Papeete, Tahiti. Presbyterian
VOCKLER, RT. REV. JOHN C. Bishop Coadjutor, Diocese of Adelaide. Formerly Vice-Warden, St. John's College, Morpeth.
Address: 11 Brougham Place, N. Adelaide, S. Australia. Anglican
WAQAIRAWAI, MR. TIMOCI. Senior circuit steward, Suva ; local preacher. Formerly schoolmaster.
Address: P.O. Box 357, Suva, Fiji. Methodist
WEBER, REV. HANS-RUEDI. Executive Secretary, Department on the Laity, World Council of Churches. Formerly missionary working for the Dutch Reformed Church in Indonesia.
Address: 17 Route de Malagnou, Geneva, Switzerland.
(*Consultant*) Presbyterian
WILLIS, MR. JOHN.
Address: c/o Union Steamship Co., Apia, W. Samoa.
Congregational
WYLLIE, MRS. MABEL G. Lecturer in anthropology, Dept. of Tutorial Classes, Univ. of Sydney and Australian School for Ecumenical Mission ; member, Board of Methodist Overseas Missions ; treasurer, National Missionary Council of Australia.
Address: Wesley College, Newtown, New South Wales, Australia.
(*Consultant*) Methodist
ZIO, REV. JOEL. Minister, Methodist Church in the Solomon Islands.
Address: Methodist Mission, Munda, British Solomon Islands.
Methodist

TOMA, REV. VAVAE. Secretary, Local Arrangements Committee.
Address: P.O. Box 468, Apia, W. Samoa.

Allocation to Commissions

Commission A – The Ministry

Tuilovoni, Rev. S. (M) (Fiji) – *Chairman*
Gaius, Rev. Saimon (M) (New Guinea)
Gribble, Rev. C. F. (M) (Australia)
Kabel, Rev. J. P. (P) (New Guinea)
Madine, Rev. Xowie (P) (New Caledonia)
Metai, Rev. Kaitara (C) (Gilbert I.)
Osborne, Rev. K. B. (B) (New Guinea)
Perry, Rev. R. (C) (New Guinea)
Pilot, Rev. Boggo (A) (Thursday I.)
Sapolu, Pastor Mila (C) (Samoa)
Vernier, Rev. H. (P) (Tahiti)
Vockler, Bp. J. C. (A) (Australia)
Newbigin, Bp. Lesslie (CSI) (I.M.C.) – *Consultant*

Commission B – The Unfinished Task of Evangelism

Fullerton, Rev. L. D. (M) (Fiji) – *Chairman*
Alafurai, Rev. L. (A) (Solomons)
Craig, Rev. C. S. (C) (London)
Duncan, Rev. D. E. (P) (New Zealand)
Hand, Bp. G. D. (A) (New Guinea)
Heine, Rev. John (C) (Marshall I.)
Kautau, Rev. Afelisi (C) (Niue)
Maloali, Rev. W. (P) (New Guinea)
Maddox, Rev. Russell (M) (Samoa)
Mileng, Mr. Stahl (L) (New Guinea)
Path, Rev. Titus (P) (New Hebrides)
Robinson, Rev. W. W. (A) (Fiji)
Soejatno, Rev. Ardi (P) (Indonesia)
Weber, Rev. H. R. (P) (W.C.C.) – *Consultant*

Commission C – The Relevance of the Gospel to Changing Conditions of Life

Horwell, Rev. A. G. (P) (New Hebrides) – *Chairman*
Ali, Mr. Sultan (M) (Fiji)
Bevilacqua, Rev. J. J. (C) (Hawaii)
Bogotu, Mr. Francis (A) (Solomons)
Guise, Mr. John (A) (New Guinea)
Jonathan, Pastor (P) (New Hebrides)
Jones, Rev. Emlyn (C) (Gilbert I.)
Kisiu, Mr. Misiel (M) (New Guinea)
Lesser, Archbishop N. A. (A) (New Zealand)
Seidenbinder, Rev. P. (P) (New Caledonia)
Stuckey, Rev. J. M. (P) (Australia)
Thorogood, Rev. B. G. (C) (Cook I.)
Willis, Mr. John (C) (Nauru)
Zio, Rev. Joel (M) (Solomons)
Orchard, Rev. R. K. (C) (I.M.C.) – *Consultant*

Commission D – The Place of Young People in the Life of the Church

Tamahori, Rev. John (A) (New Zealand) – *Chairman*
Andrews, Rev. S. G. (M) (New Zealand)
Baloiloi, Mr. Enosi (M) (New Guinea)
Barnes, Rev. R. L. (M) (New Guinea)
Bradshaw, Dr. John (C) (Samoa)
Chiu, Rev. Ban It (A) (Australia)
Cocks, Rev. N. H. F. (C) (Australia)
Ehu, Deacon T. (P) (Tahiti)
Kalapu, Mr. Luafatasage (C) (Samoa)
Marino, Mr. Joshua (C) (Caroline I.)
Mo'ungaloa, Rev. V. (M) (Tonga)
Nabwakulea, Mr. Setepano (M) (New Guinea)
Pere, Rev. Ta Upu (C) (Cook I.)
Pidjo, Rev. Tein (P) (New Caledonia)
Than, U Kyaw (B) (E.A.C.C.) – *Consultant*

Commission E – The Christian Family

Mataafa, Mrs. Fetaui (C) (Samoa) – *Chairman*
Cowled, Rev. S. G. C. (M) (Fiji)
Frerichs, Dr. A. C. (L) (New Guinea)
Hanlin, Dr. Harold (C) (Caroline I.)
Iotama, Rev. Seve (C) (Ellice I.)
Ledoux, Rev. Marc-André (P) (New Caledonia)
Mailei, Mr. Tala (M) (Samoa)
Mea, Pastor Retau (C) (New Guinea)
Raapoto, Rev. S. (P) (Tahiti)
Rawcliffe, Archdeacon D. A. (A) (New Hebrides)
Waqairawai, Mr. Timoci (M) (Fiji)
Wyllie, Mrs. M. G. (M) (Australia) – *Consultant*

(Observers' names are italicized
  A = Anglican
  B = Baptist
  C = Congregational
CSI = Church of South India
  L = Lutheran
  M = Methodist
  P = Presbyterian or Reformed)

[2]